A central part of every Christian faith and Christlike character. Hotsenpiller will guide you through this pro- cess by imparting scriptural insights and practical steps to partner with the Holy Spirit for lasting change. Your prayer life is about to get an upgrade as you tap into the greater things of God through fasting!

—Dr. Ché Ahn
Senior Leader, Harvest Rock Church
President, Harvest International Ministry
International Chancellor, Wagner University

I'm so thankful for my friendship with Tammy Hotsen- piller! She is an incredible encourager and a prayer war- rior. I have been inspired in my own life by Tammy's commitment to prayer and fasting. In her latest book, *Fasting for a Change,* she brings insight, wisdom, the fruit of her studies, and experience. If you have felt like you've been hitting dead ends, pick up this book! It's time for a change!

—Kim Walker-Smith
Singer, Writer, Worship Leader, Jesus Culture
Music

Fasting is something that every believer should under- stand but it has become a lost art. Tammy has provided something that I desperately need and I know you do too. Through *Fasting for a Change,* she has created teaching and inspiration that will create faith to fast for purpose and a hunger in you to use this powerful tool of fasting. This book is a must-have before you engage in your next individual or corporate fast. You will have something that can really lead you through this important choice you are making that is biblically sound and anointed of God.

—Shawn Bolz
Host, *The Shawn Bolz Show* and *Exploring the Marketplace*
Author, *Translating God* and *Encounter*

Pastor Tammy exemplifies the role of a devoted intercessor and mother for our generation. Her unwavering commitment to fasting, prayer, and imparting these practices to the next generation is making a profound impact on the lives of young people today. I highly recommend her book *Fasting for a Change* as a valuable resource that will equip you with everything you need to experience God's transformative breakthroughs in your own life.

—Brian Barcelona
President and CEO, One Voice Student Missions

In her new book, *Fasting for a Change*, Tammy Hotsenpiller once again teaches and coaches us through fasting for the next level of change. This third book on fasting takes us to a deeper understanding of spiritual fasting so we will achieve the abundant life Jesus came to bring us (John 10:10)!

Tammy believes that "fasting is a vital key to our success in winning the war with both our flesh and our enemy." We agree! In this last-days battle that we are in right now, believers must use every spiritual weapon God has given us; fasting is a powerful one! If you want to operate from a place of being all that He created you to be, you must get hold of *Fasting for a Change*, read it, and let Tammy coach you through fasting and prayer to make the course corrections you need to have life abundantly!

—Jim and Lori Bakker
Hosts, *The Jim Bakker Show*

Once again, Tammy brings new insights and wisdom to fasting. If you are looking for breakthrough and personal change, you will find the resources in this book. I believe the exercise of fasting combined with the power of prayer unlocks the divine realm. Change is a part of personal growth, and in her new book, *Fasting for a Change*, Tammy will lead you step by step in becoming all God created you to be.

—SEAN FEUCHT
AUTHOR, MISSIONARY, ARTIST, ACTIVIST, AND FOUNDER
OF LET US WORSHIP

Whether you're new to fasting or you want to fine-tune your fasting plan, this is the fasting manual to help you to have change in your life! Whether your goal is to sharpen your fasting knowledge or to see God move and the breakthrough come your way, *Fasting for a Change* is your answer! I am a fasting expert, and I couldn't put this book down! *Fasting for a Change* is the best companion for your journey!

—CHANTEL RAY-FINCH
AUTHOR, FASTING COACH, AND CEO OF CANZELL

FASTING
—— FOR A ——
CHANGE

TAMMY HOTSENPILLER

**CHARISMA
HOUSE**

Cataloging-in-Publication Data is on file with the Library of Congress.
International Standard Book Number: 978-1-63641-269-6
E-book ISBN: 978-1-63641-270-2

1 2023

Printed in the United States of America

Most Charisma Media products are available at special quantity discounts for bulk purchase for sales promotions, premiums, fund-raising, and educational needs. For details, call us at (407) 333-0600 or visit our website at www.charismamedia.com.

This book is dedicated to my mother, a woman who was not afraid to change. Through pain, setbacks, difficulties, and adversity, she never stopped growing and blessing the lives of others. This book is for those who are ready to change—ready to leave the past behind and embrace new beginnings.

CONTENTS

Week One:
Fasting With Moses

DAY 01
FASTING FOR CONFIDENCE

DAY 02
FASTING FOR DETERMINATION

DAY 03
FASTING FOR COURAGE

DAY 04
FASTING FOR FAITH

DAY 05
FASTING FOR CONTENTMENT

Week Two:
Fasting With Elijah

Week Three:
Fasting With Jesus

WORDS CANNOT EXPRESS my appreciation for all those who made this book possible.

Thank you, Diane Campos, for your diligent eye in editing and combing through every detail in this book.

Thank you, Lisa Haines, for your passionate edits and for standing by my side with encouragement along the way.

Thank you to Charisma Media. It has been an honor to work on what is now my third fasting book with you. Your passion and encouragement for each of your authors are a gift beyond words.

Thank you to my family, who has always supported and encouraged me in every endeavor I've taken.

Thank you to Influence Church for always being the first to engage in fasting and believing God for miracles.

May God bless you as you read this book and exercise your faith to see personal change.

ACKNOWLEDGMENTS

MAYBE YOU'VE WONDERED, "Is fasting right for me?" or, "How do I fast, and what are the rules?" Maybe you are simply curious about biblical fasting, or maybe desperation and longing has you looking for a change in your life. Either way, I am excited you've picked up this book.

Because I have written and taught extensively about fasting, people ask me often (a) if fasting really works and (b) if God expects us to fast as Christians. My answer is *yes* and *yes*. All of life is warfare, and fasting is a two-part strategy God put in place to help His followers win the battle with the enemy.

There is a kind of general understanding in Christian culture that practices like prayer, worship, and Bible reading are critical to spiritual health. But the Gospels give us an open secret hidden in plain sight, somehow obscured in Western culture, that while prayer, Scripture, hymns, and choruses are all helpful, they are not enough. There are some battles in our lives that will not be won through those disciplines alone no matter how hard or long we pray, how much Scripture we memorize or meditate on, or how many songs we sing.

When the disciples were trying to heal a boy of a demonic spirit and were unsuccessful, Jesus responded in Matthew 17:21, "However, this kind does not go out except by prayer and fasting." Prayer is always powerful, but there are times when prayer in and of itself is not enough. There are some realities in our lives that are simply not going to shift without both prayer *and* fasting.

We fight spiritual battles on two primary fronts:

the war with our flesh, and the war with our enemy. Fasting is crucial to winning them both. As we walk this path of spiritual change together, if you are new to fasting or have questions about the various fasts in the Bible, please visit my website, TammyHotsenpiller. com, for examples and teachings on why we fast and how to fast. There you will find detailed instructions and examples on how to choose a biblical fast. You can also join me each morning for your daily coaching video.

As your fasting coach, I will lead you day by day to help you stay strong and complete your fast successfully.

Congratulations on seeing God move. Breakthrough is coming your way.

—TAMMY

A FIELD GUIDE FOR CHANGE

SOMETIMES IT TAKES a crisis in our lives to push us into a new spiritual realm. Desperation is often the catalyst for breakthrough. It was 2013 when I found myself in need of a miracle. I had heard about fasting, and of course I'd read about fasting in the Bible, but it had never been a part of my own spiritual practice. I was out of answers, and nothing else I tried was working. I had nowhere else to go but to God.

Prayer had been such an integral part of the story of our church and of my life to that point—but looking back, I see how I was in the same place the disciples were in Matthew 17: the place where prayer alone is just not enough. They were facing a spirit that was deeply embedded inside of this boy—the way habits, addictions, patterns, and cycles can be deeply embedded in our lives now. When we come against those areas of deepest resistance, prayer alone will not bring breakthrough. It is going to take a supernatural act of faith, along with spiritual discipline, to unlock the power that we need.

That story penetrated my heart like never before. I had been a prayer warrior for many years, but I had not yet combined the discipline of fasting with praying for my answer. As a pastor and spiritual leader of a local congregation, I knew I had to go deeper. I had to lead our church on a spiritual fast.

Out of this journey, I wrote my first fasting book in 2020, *Fasting With God*. As it always is when we fast, it was not just a time to do without but a time to go further into the things of God. I walked

1

our church through twenty-one days of the names of God. As we meditated on the divine names, we fasted and prayed, going deep into the Word of God. I wrote my second fasting book, *Fasting for Miracles*, the following year. That marked a season where fasting propelled us into a supernatural realm of believing God for those things that we could not see. We fasted, believed, and sought the supernatural realm to become our reality.

> God has given you the practice of fasting not as a burden but as a gift to unlock the transformation your soul already cries out for.

But with research comes growth, so now ten years after I began this transformational fasting journey, I find that I am not done with it—and God is not done unlocking these truths in me. The more I delve into the Word of God, the more I realize that fasting is meant to be an ongoing spiritual discipline that we develop. While we often discover fasting out of desperation, it should not be just a last-resort option. While we may encounter fasting during some called, consecrated season, it is not just seasonal. It is intended to be a regular part of the rhythm of our lives.

In today's culture intermittent fasting is encouraged. Through social media, personal platforms, podcasts, and preaching, the health benefits of intermittent fasting have become a hot topic. I agree that our physical bodies need intermittent fasting and that there are physical benefits to cleansing our temples. God created us to fast—He created us to sleep and then to wake up each morning and break our fast. God knew our bodies need time to repair and rest. The health benefits of intermittent fasting, too, point to the brilliance of the Creator and the wisdom of this practice He has given to us. Yet while I personally practice intermittent fasting for my physical well-being, it is *not the same thing* as a spiritual fast.

During this ten-year journey with fasting, it has become clear to me that the fast we are intended to engage in is not just the kind that is good for our bodies. We are meant to practice biblical fasting. Biblical fasting may certainly bring the same benefits of rest, clarity, and physical well-being as other fasts, but it entails another dimension of this practice. In both the Old Testament and the New Testament, God shows us that fasting is also a practice of spiritual warfare. It doesn't just enhance our sleep and speed up our metabolism; it gives us the discipline to know how to say no to our flesh and yes to God. Biblical fasting empowers us to suppress our cravings and turn to Christ for our answers.

No wonder after writing two books on fasting I have found that God is not finished with me yet. As I practice and coach my clients, I believe we are holistic beings; this is a biblical truth: we are body, we are soul, and we are spirit.

This is what it is, in the language of Genesis, to be made in the image of the God who is Father, Son, and Holy Spirit. We, too, are body and soul and spirit, so all three of these compartments of our lives need to be stewarded well. My physical body needs the practice of intermittent fasting. My spirit needs to engage the supernatural realm through a biblical fast. But what about my soul? I like to define the soul as our mind, our will, and our emotions—the decision-making mechanism God placed within humanity to operate in this world.

It is this craving of the soul for the kind of change that can be brought about only by fasting that brings us here now.

We need to seek God in prayer and fasting for the personal growth and development that we want and need. We need to ask God to show us the areas in our lives in which we are not yet all that He created us to be.

Are there aspects of your life that you know need to change, but up until now it has seemed impossible? You are not alone. God has given you the practice of fasting not as a burden but as a gift to unlock the transformation your soul already cries out for.

TO MAKE NEW AND TO REPLACE

Whether you have had a little or a lot of experience with fasting, I am certain you have had plenty of experience with trying to change. We are fascinated by the idea of change, the prospect of change— and we are also often terrified by the upheaval that change brings. Change entails both making something different and also replacing something that already exists with something else. No wonder it is both exhilarating and terrifying to consider change: we do, in fact, long for *newness*. But we don't create the new that we seek in a vacuum; to change is also to replace something that came before. To get to the new, we must undergo a process of confronting and clearing out the old to carve out space for the better.

Almost everyone wants to change, *theoretically*—or at minimum wants the fruit of the results that change would bring. Yet why does it seem that many of us never actually experience the change our souls yearn for?

As a life coach and pastor, I have worked with countless people who told me they want to change, that they have tried to change, but never see the results. While the particulars of the stories change, the narrative is always the same. Consistently, I have found that people don't experience change because they lack three things: desire, discipline, and accountability. Desire is the *fuel* for change, the energy that gets us moving forward. Discipline is the *practice* of change, or we might say *practices*—the concrete habits we form that facilitate transformation. Accountability provides the *structure* for change, giving us the support we need to cultivate these habits until we create the newness we seek.

Desire, discipline, and accountability can be ominous words—deep down we know that to embrace them is to become something very different from what we have been, and we always fear the unknown. So why would we change, then, when change can feel like such a threat to whatever little sense of order we have? Even if our lives aren't exactly "working," there is real appeal to the familiar—a reason we often choose "the devil we know"!

But you can and must change, because you know in the deepest part of your soul that there is no other way. You know that anger, alcohol, fear, bitterness, jealousy, and pride are keeping you from the life God wants for you, the life you most deeply want for yourself. In some cases you may know that you must change because others have pointed it out in your life. But on some level, the real reason any of us seek meaningful change, however else we know that we need it, is because God Himself has convicted us of the need.

That still, small voice that summons you to change is not the only one you hear, is it? When you start this journey, inevitably you will hear the voice inside you that says, "Can I really change?" After all, you've tried this before. You've experienced the starts and stops, the humiliation of not following through on a goal. Can you really change this time?

Yes. Yes, you can. Not because of the greatness of your willpower but because the One who wills this change for you is great. Jesus said in John 10:10, "I have come that they may have life, and that they may have it more abundantly." The Lord of the church Himself has said that you can and should have an abundant life and that He wants to give it to you. You can change—not only because it is what you desire, but because Christ desires it for you and in you.

Sure, we have many reasons to resist change, all the reasons that we have resisted it before. We resist change because

- we cannot fully imagine a life that different from the one we have—again, we fear the unknown;

- we simply have not cultivated the habits necessary for change before—we are undisciplined;

- on some level we have become at home with the habits we do have, even if they are bad ones—we are comfortable with our way of life; and

- even if we don't exactly love the way things are, precisely because we have lived this way for so long, on some level even our "want to" gets broken—we outright lack personal desire.

For all the resistance you have felt, all the times you've tried and failed before, even so, you know that this time *really is the time for a change*! It's time for a one-eighty! It's time to seek God and ask Him to bring about the changes for you and in you that only He can.

Like the disciples, you have some things in your life that aren't going to go out any other way but through prayer and fasting. Whether it is a sin or a stronghold you need to eliminate, or self-discipline that you need to cultivate, we all need a change in our lives. We have to change, ultimately, because we simply realize we cannot continue down the same path, that the way we are living is no longer sustainable for us.

Maybe you need a breakthrough, a burden lifted, or a blessing. In any case, you know you need a *real change* in your life.

** CAUTION **

The precise reason many of us have experienced so much frustration trying to engineer change for ourselves is that we have attempted to rely on our own power to change. It is very important that I explain the importance of not confusing your ability and strengths with those of God alone.

We will discuss several characteristics and behavioral traits we all long to discover and develop in our personal lives. That said, only through Christ alone can we truly be all God created us to be. This workbook is not designed to teach you how to muster up the strength or knowledge to make changes on your own, but to help you learn to embrace and encounter the power of the living God so that you can "do all things through Christ who strengthens [you]" (Phil. 4:13). Never confuse what you can do with what only God can do.

WE ALL HAVE A CHOICE

Personalities and behaviors are an interesting combination. You look at someone who is carefree, driven, successful, and always positive and ask yourself, "Were they just born that way?"

There are some people who just naturally have the Midas touch. They come out of the womb seemingly destined for success and prosperity. Then, of course, we all know there are those who seem to always have a life of drama and difficulty. They just can't seem to get a break. It's one thing after another.

Is this destiny, or is this a decision?

I, for one, am an optimist. Maybe that's why I became a life coach—I see the good and the possibility in just about everything. When difficulty comes along or an obstacle presents itself, my first thought is, "How do we fix this? How do we change the outcome?"

The reality is that we all have a choice. We can make a choice to do something different than we have done before, to be something different and something more than what we have been before. We have the opportunity to grow and learn and develop and to truly become the people God created us to be.

In this book, *Fasting for a Change*, we are going to look at the characteristics and behaviors that bring joy, peace, and fulfillment, which I believe is God's desire for each of us.

This is a two-part study. First we'll look at the things you can do—the changes you can make and the decisions and effort it will take on your part to bring about a change. Then we will combine these efforts with the spiritual discipline of fasting. This break-through power can only come by the supernatural hand of God.

Fasting for a Change will help you identify the areas of growth and personal development you desperately desire. Healthy habits and positive characteristics lead you to become the person God created you to be. Healthy choices combined with spiritual fasting are the two-edged sword you need in order to see your breakthrough and to become your personal best.

There are several keys to personal growth and spiritual maturity, and they all begin with a desire and discipline for individual change. I want to invite you to go on a journey with me, a journey along the pathway to becoming your *best self*.

In this twenty-one-day workbook you will come face to face with your strengths and your weaknesses. Coming to terms with one is not more important or more necessary than coming to terms with the other. You will learn about biblical figures just like you and me who also had to make daily decisions to become their best selves. Through the prism of their stories we will explore twenty-one key qualities that make every human being the ideal version of themselves.

Each day you will contemplate a portion of Scripture that addresses the day's key characteristic as well as glean lessons on fasting from three biblical figures: Moses, Elijah, and Jesus. I also encourage you to visit my website, TammyHotsenpiller.com, for daily coaching videos designed to encourage you through your fast.

The stories of the men and women we read about in Scripture are constituted the same way all of our stories are—their lives were a series of decisions and choices. Your life now is a series of decisions and choices. With that in view, then, let me ask you, Are you ready to look inside your heart and contemplate the hard questions?

Do you need to change?

Is it time for a change?

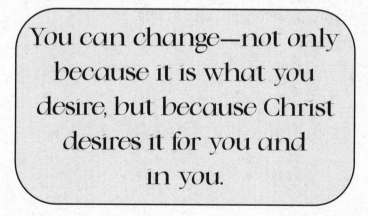

You can change—not only because it is what you desire, but because Christ desires it for you and in you.

The twenty-one healthy characteristics we will explore in this book will give us a road map for change. You may already possess some of these to a certain degree, but please keep an open heart and make room for improvement. We all have space for personal growth and expansion if we are willing to embrace change. There is so much more in you.

This is not a collection of ideas; this is a field guide for change. You yourself are a workbook, and the Spirit of God is ready to tell a new story of your life. So let's not just engage this with our heads; let's actually get started fasting for *a change*.

Since this book is not an intellectual discourse about fasting but an invitation to bring those longings into the presence of God, I invite you to stop now and pray this prayer along with me:

> *Father God, I ask for patience through this process. I ask, Holy Spirit, that You temper my heart. Show me with divine eyes the areas in my life I need to change—the places I can grow and expand in my personal life. I ask You to lead and guide me on this journey.*
>
> *Give me the strength to make course corrections where needed. Accept my fast, and my prayer, as an offering unto You, and speak to me as only You can. In Jesus' name, amen.*

week one

FASTING WITH MOSES

As we begin our journey together, we will look at Israel's story for a glimpse of the kind of determination we will need to move forward. Fasting is a discipline that helps us get out of bondage. What better place to start than with the man who led the people of God out of Egyptian bondage through the exodus?

SCRIPTURE PASSAGES

When I went up into the mountain to receive the tablets of stone, the tablets of the covenant which the LORD made with you, then I remained on the mountain forty days and forty nights. I did not eat bread or drink water. The LORD delivered to me two tablets of stone, written with the finger of God, and on them was written all the words which the LORD spoke to you at the mountain out of the midst of the fire on the day of the assembly.

At the end of forty days and forty nights, the LORD gave me the two tablets of stone, the tablets of the covenant. Then the LORD said to me, "Arise, go down from here quickly, for your people whom you brought out of Egypt have corrupted themselves. They are quickly turned aside from the way which I commanded them. They have made a molded image for themselves."

Furthermore the LORD spoke to me, saying, "I have seen this people, and indeed, they are a stubborn people. Let Me alone, so that I may destroy them and blot out their name from under heaven, and I will make of you a nation mightier and greater than they."

So I returned and came down from the mount, and the mount burned with fire, and the two tablets of the covenant were in my two hands. I looked, and indeed, you had sinned against the Lord your God and had made yourselves a molded calf. You had quickly turned aside out of the way which the Lord had commanded you. I took the two tablets and threw them out of my two hands and broke them before your eyes.

—Deuteronomy 9:9–17, MEV

At that time the Lord said to me, "Cut out for yourself two tablets of stone like the first and come up to Me onto the mountain and make an ark of wood for yourself. I will write on the tablets the words that were on the first tablets which you broke, and you shall put them in the ark."

So I made an ark of acacia wood and cut out two tablets of stone just like the first and went up onto the mountain with the two tablets in my hand. He wrote on the tablets just like the first writing, the Ten Commandments which the Lord spoke to you at the mountain out of the midst of the fire on the day of the assembly, and the Lord gave them to me. I turned around and came down from the mountain and put the tablets in the ark which I had made, and there they are, just as the Lord commanded me.

—Deuteronomy 10:1–5, MEV

GOING DEEPER

Moses was chosen by God to lead the children of Israel out of captivity. Most of us know the story of how he confidently stood in front of Pharaoh, saying, "Let my people go."

The granting of the release for the children of Israel to be set free would soon be recanted as Pharaoh realized what he had just done. "These are my slaves and workmen, my bakers, and my house-keepers. Go after them," he demanded.

The people of God go, and the Egyptians go after them. This is the beginning of the Israelites' journey through the wilderness. As it is for all of us, this journey of change was not an arbitrary deci-sion—the Israelites, like us, were dislodged, forced out. They had to call out to God because they had no other choice.

God heard the cries of His people, and the Israelites made their way to the Red Sea, feeling empowered and free—but the victory would be short-lived. As they turned around, the army of Pharaoh was hot on their heels, and they were surrounded on either side. Yet as in all our journeys with God, He was with them. They crossed the sea with confidence with the Spirit of God as their guide. This was just the first of many desperate encounters the children of Israel would have, for there was a vast wilderness in front of them—as you may feel there is a vast wilderness that stretches in front of you now.

God provided the Israelites with His presence with a cloud by day and a flame of fire by night, but the people still resorted to grumbling and complaining. Although He sent daily manna and provided them with water along the way, along with many spiritual encounters, they still bickered. Though they tasted their freedom in the wild, finally out from under the tyranny of Egypt, they regretted their decision to leave. "Why should we be free in the wil-derness when we could be in bondage in Egypt?" they asked. Have you ever chosen the familiarity of something that held you captive over the wild, terrible danger of freedom? At least we knew what to expect in Egypt.

As their leader, Moses knew he needed help from God. It was now time for him to find out just why he had been chosen. It was time for a mountaintop experience. As he approached the tip of Mount Sinai, Moses met God face to face.

There Moses sat still for forty days, hearing from the heart of God while the commandments for the people of Israel were spoken to him directly. This became what we know as *the Moses Fast*—a time when Moses abstained from food to hear the word of the Lord. There is no earthly food that can compare with the bread of heaven, the nourishment of revelation.

After receiving the Ten Commandments from God, Moses was released to go down the mountain and share them with the Israelites. But as you may know, when Moses entered the camp he found the people's hearts had grown cold and they were singing and dancing while worshipping foreign gods.

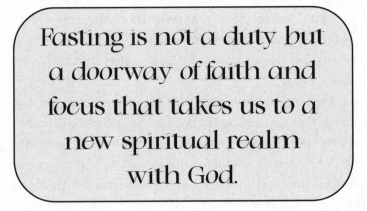

Fasting is not a duty but a doorway of faith and focus that takes us to a new spiritual realm with God.

The very thing the Israelites had left Egypt for they had now re-created in the wilderness. Sound familiar?

Moses responded out of his humanity by throwing the tablets on the ground in disbelief and disgust—a reminder of how quickly we can go from being in the presence of God to engaging our flesh through anger and disappointment. That was an act born of frustration and incredulity, and now Moses would have to learn a valuable lesson about humility. Back up the mountain he went for take two of the Ten Commandments.

Once again fasting for forty days, Moses sat in the presence of God, this time going even deeper. Fasting will do that—it will take you into the depths. Your desires will move from the things of this world to the things of God. Your cravings and pleasures are suppressed, denied, and controlled in exchange for a higher desire, that of breakthrough, freedom, connection, and intimacy with God. The trouble with so many of our desires before the fast is that they are superficial longings for comfort, familiarity, or escape. When we fast, we finally tap into the deepest desires of our souls. We may not be eating physical bread, but we can finally eat freely of the bread of life that truly satisfies.

Fasting is a spiritual discipline. It is a choice we make to suppress our flesh, those top-level desires that never serve us well, and to wait on God. Fasting was never meant to be something we do pridefully or out of obligation; it is simply a gate to take us deeper. Fasting is not a duty but a doorway of faith and focus that takes us to a new spiritual realm with God.

In our first week together we will look at healthy characteristics we all long to possess in our personal lives. These are qualities and disciplines that bring us into alignment with God and out of alignment with the ways of the world—those ways that, as it was for the Israelites in Egypt, have enslaved rather than liberated us. There are all kinds of things we can do that generally benefit our bodies and minds, but fasting is unique in that it actually facilitates freedom. This book will lead you through a twenty-one-day journey to becoming the person God sees you to be.

Take time and read through the Moses Fast this week. Note the ways God met Moses on that forty-day journey. Ask God to give you the strength and the discipline to stay focused on your twenty-one-day fast.

Make sure you join me each morning for our coaching videos. These will help you to stay accountable and encourage you through the process.

FOR FURTHER STUDY

Take a few moments to prayerfully meditate on the following verses as we prepare for the first week of the fast. Note just how significant fasting was for God's people during the most formational years of Israel's history. These are formational years for you too. When the fast feels difficult, it is important to remember just how crucial this practice has always been in the process of God's people becoming free.

- Deuteronomy 9:9
- Exodus 24:18
- Deuteronomy 9:18
- Exodus 34:28

COACHING THOUGHTS

As we work through this week's healthy characteristics, we will ground these reflections in Moses' forty-day fast. We will see how God meets us in our time of sacrifice to grow our faith and increase our reliance upon Him.

These exercises will help you take these concepts and contextualize them in your own personal life and thus are as important as any of the content. With that in view, take your time and work through each coaching concept and discussion question. This process is key to your self-discovery and personal growth.

day
01

FASTING FOR
CONFIDENCE

ADAM & EVE

There is no worse screen to block out the Spirit

than confidence in our own intelligence.

—JOHN CALVIN

con·fi·dence | ˈkän-fə-dən(t)s |

noun

the feeling or belief that one can rely on someone or something: firm trust

the state of feeling certain about the truth of something

SIGNS OF LACK OF CONFIDENCE

- It's hard for you to receive a compliment.
- You see your mistakes more than you see your successes.
- You feel like you are less than others.
- You compare yourself to others.
- Your happiness depends on others.

BUILDING SELF-CONFIDENCE IS a growing trend in today's culture. Coaches, seminars, businesses, and even churches are paving the way for a "new and improved" you. Try this method or that routine, and voilà! There you have it: self-confidence. The problem is that the focus is on you and not on the God that lives in you. Don't get me wrong: I have attended seminars and even hosted self-esteem workshops. But we will only know the depth of our security and confidence when we come face to face with our Maker, the Creator, God Himself. This is the kind of confidence Paul wrote about in Philippians 1:6: "Being confident of this very thing, that He who has begun a good work in you will complete it until the day of Jesus Christ."

SCRIPTURE PASSAGES

The world has only changed so much. In the very beginning of Scripture we have an account of the first humans, who were fully dependent on God, fully confident in God's provision—lacking nothing. Yet even though they had everything they needed, they were tempted to draw their confidence from elsewhere. As you read this ancient story, keep an open mind and see if you can find your own story in it.

Then God said, "Let us make man in our image, after our likeness, and let them have dominion over the fish of the sea, and over the birds of the air, and over the livestock, and over all the earth, and over every creeping thing that creeps on the earth."

So God created man in His own image; in the image of God He created him; male and female He created them. God blessed them and said to them, "Be fruitful and multiply, and replenish the earth and subdue it. Rule over the fish of the sea and over the birds of the air and over every living thing that moves on the earth."

Then God said, "See, I have given you every plant yielding seed which is on the face of all the earth and every tree which has fruit yielding seed. It shall be food for you."

—GENESIS 1:26–29, MEV

The LORD God took the man and put him in the garden of Eden to till it and to keep it. And the LORD God commanded the man, saying, "Of every tree of the garden you may freely eat, but of the tree of the knowledge of good and evil you shall not eat, for in the day that you eat from it you will surely die."

Then the LORD God said, "It is not good that the man should be alone. I will make him a helper suitable for him."

Out of the ground the LORD God formed every beast of the field and every bird of the sky, and brought them to the man to see what he would call them. Whatever the man called every living creature, that was its name. The man gave names to all the livestock, to the birds of the sky, and to every beast of the field, but for Adam there was not found a helper suitable for him.

So the Lord God caused a deep sleep to fall on Adam, and he slept. Then He took one of his ribs and closed up the place with flesh. Then the rib which the Lord God had taken from man, He made into a woman, and He brought her to the man. Then Adam said, "This is now bone of my bones and flesh of my flesh; she will be called Woman, for she was taken out of Man."

—Genesis 2:15–23, MEV

Now the serpent was more subtle than any beast of the field which the Lord God had made. And he said to the woman, "Has God said, 'You shall not eat of any tree of the garden'?"

And the woman said to the serpent, "We may eat of the fruit from the trees of the garden; but from the fruit of the tree which is in the midst of the garden, God has said, 'You will not eat of it, nor will you touch it, or else you will die.'"

Then the serpent said to the woman, "You surely will not die! For God knows that on the day you eat of it your eyes will be opened and you will be like God, knowing good and evil."

When the woman saw that the tree was good for food, that it was pleasing to the eyes and a tree desirable to make one wise, she took of its fruit and ate; and she gave to her husband with her, and he ate. Then the eyes of both were opened, and they knew that they were naked. So they sewed fig leaves together and made coverings for themselves.

Then they heard the sound of the Lord God walking in the garden in the cool of the day, and the man and his wife hid themselves from the presence of the Lord God among the trees of the garden.

—Genesis 3:1–8, MEV

GOING DEEPER

God began a good work in Adam and Eve. He gave them everything they needed. Along with knowing they were loved and protected by the hand of God, they had the confidence that every need they would ever have had already been met—and the serpent knew it. The enemy always attacks the confidence we have in Christ. He tries to rob and steal and destroy our self-worth, to make us question the very God who created us.

So much of the world we confront now is contained in this garden image. We are still staring down the same choices. Once again, the enemy would love to target these areas in our lives—to make us gods of our own making.

Why is this temptation so alluring? Adam and Eve lacked nothing. God provided every resource, every relationship, every remedy they would need for life. The only limitation God put on Adam and Eve was a tree in the middle of the garden to stay away from: the tree of the knowledge of good and evil. God did not want to place upon humanity the decision of right versus wrong, good versus evil, and do versus don't. That was not God's plan. His plan was love and unity, confidence and freedom.

It is impossible to trust God and play God at the same time. God created us not for control but for trust, yet ultimately He gave the gift of free will to His creation as a gift of love. Love does not coerce or control. It is because God loves us that He gave each of us that same free will. Day by day, moment by moment each of us has the free will to choose our destiny and our decisions.

What if Adam and Eve had used the confidence God gave them to stand against the serpent and those demonic powers? What if their personal confidence was so strong that they spoke back to the lies that were coming their way? Confidence is the ability to know who you are—to stand strong on the stage of life with the mindset that you are enough, knowing you are a creation made in the image of the almighty God.

My only warning to you, my friend, is this: do not allow your confidence in God to turn into arrogance in yourself.

Several years ago I sat in the audience eager to hear a message from a well-known keynote speaker. She, in my mind, was a true leader—a woman of integrity and godliness. She was poised, beautiful, and very well dressed.

I remember the moment she walked on the stage. I was so attracted by her presentation because this was a woman who walked in confidence and not arrogance. There is a vast difference between the two, you know. A person who walks in confidence knows his or her identity comes through Christ. A person who walks in arrogance thinks his or her identity comes from himself or herself. Arrogance is really just a manifestation of fear, an attempt to mask the fact that we are afraid and have false confidence grounded only in a sense of self.

On the other hand, fear can also cause us to cower and not even attempt to do what God has called us to do. The only way the enemy can steal your confidence is through intimidation.

My husband is not only the love of my life, but he also carries a sense of charisma that fills every room. When we were first married, I was so excited to journey with him through seminary and on into our first several pastorates, but the truth was I felt intimidated by his strength, charisma, and knowledge. There were many times when I simply felt less than perfect. I was his wife and the mother of his children—you know, "the preacher's wife."

Although I knew I had gifts and talents, I had not yet developed or embraced my abilities. I didn't operate in arrogance but in the other direction fear will take you: I stayed silent in the shell of motherhood and marriage. The few times I had opportunities to speak, I would diligently prepare. Although I knew I was adequate, I still walked in my husband's shadow.

I remember having my Bible study one morning when 2 Corinthians 3:5 leapt off the page into my heart: "Not that we are sufficient of ourselves to think of anything as being from ourselves, but our sufficiency is from God." What? I read it again and heard the Lord say, "Your adequacy is not in you, Tammy; your adequacy, your ability, your confidence is in Me, Jesus—your leader, your life, your Lord." The reality that I truly had gifts and abilities was now set like cement in my soul.

The problem is that knowing truth and exercising truth are two different things. It took me many years to step into my ability. But I can tell you today I am not the woman I was. That's what happens when you embrace change, when you look to God for your confidence and adequacy.

Now after years of coaching Fortune 500 companies, traveling the world, writing books, and starting companies, I can speak from experience about what making the right changes in your life can do. Having confidence in God to do all He has promised to do is the first step toward feeling competent and worthy, and that first step will change all the ones that follow.

FOR FURTHER STUDY

Prayerfully meditate on the following passages, allowing yourself to see where and how God invites us to find confidence. Sit with these verses long enough to allow them to go into the deep places in your life. Let them become your own reasons to trust, right here and right now.

- Proverbs 3:26
- Isaiah 41:10

- 2 Corinthians 3:5
- 1 John 3:20–21
- Romans 15:13
- Philippians 4:13
- Hebrews 13:6

COACHING STEPS

1. Know that you were created in the image of God. Your confidence does not come from your ability but from Him, the gift giver Himself. You can be confident in knowing He has created you in His image for good works. Stop right now and thank God for the confidence you have in being a son or daughter of God.

2. Know your enemy. The enemy will continue to try to deceive you, to tempt you with the apple of identity—to trick you and deceive you into thinking you have nothing to offer. Stand strong against the lies of your adversary. Now, think of two or three ways the enemy has lied to you. Replace those thoughts with the truth that you are protected and provided for by the hand of God.

3. Memorize the Word of God. This is how you grow in your confidence—to speak life and not death over your steps, to walk in confidence and not arrogance. The key to spiritual success, as we see in the life of Jesus Himself when He was tempted in the wilderness, is Scripture memorization. In the words of

Psalm 119:11, "Thy word have I hid in my heart, that I might not sin against thee" (KJV).

Let me encourage you to take time today to grow your confidence. Make a personal change in your life and move from arrogance and self-sufficiency to spiritual strength and confidence.

THE MOSES FAST

Moses needed to have confidence in God that he was on the right path. God had spoken to him from a burning bush and said He would be with him and not forsake him. Although his journey of faith was difficult at times, his confidence in an all-knowing and all-loving God kept him secure.

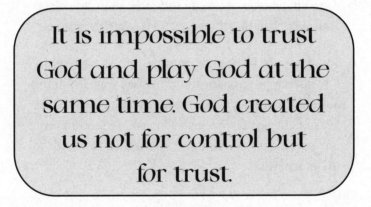

It is impossible to trust God and play God at the same time. God created us not for control but for trust.

Fasting for forty days kept Moses focused and in relationship with God. Remember, the number forty means testing in Hebrew. This was a test that would prove, not only to Moses but to all of Israel, that you can put your trust and confidence in Yahweh. Moses had to shut out the lies of the enemy telling him he was a failure and not really a leader. It is only when we take control of our conversations with the enemy that we can ever win the battle. God proved sufficient to Moses, and Moses saw the mighty hand of God move.

DISCUSSION QUESTIONS

- Have you ever stopped to consider that your confidence actually comes from God? If you have not, take a moment now and thank God for the blessing of knowing He will never leave you or forsake you. Memorize today's scripture and make it a part of your twenty-one-day fast.

- Do you struggle to feel adequate? List the areas in your life where you need God to be your adequacy. Now ask Him to fill you with His Spirit.

- Today we are fasting for confidence. As we read in our fasting passage for today, Moses was on Mount Sinai for forty days, fasting for intimacy with God. Let's begin our fast together by asking God to build our confidence in Him and strengthen our faith for the journey.

PRAYER

Dear Lord, thank You for the watchful care and protection You give me every day. I understand that my confidence and my adequacy come from You alone. Teach me to lean on You for my daily decisions and to submit to Your promptings in my heart. You have plans to give me hope and not harm. In Jesus' name, amen.

JOURNAL ENTRY

day
02

FASTING FOR
DETERMINATION

— NEHEMIAH —

Things great have small beginnings. Every downpour is just a raindrop; every fire is just a spark; every harvest is just a seed; every journey is just a step because without that step there will be no journey; without that raindrop there can be no shower; without that seed there can be no harvest.

—WILLIAM WILBERFORCE

de·ter·mi·na·tion | di-ˌtər-mə-ˈnā-shən |

noun

firmness of purpose; resoluteness

SIGNS OF LACK OF DETERMINATION

- You look for reasons and ways to quit.
- You don't have a clear plan of action.
- You are not 100 percent sure of the plan.
- You are lazy.
- Other people want something for you more than you do.

WHY IS DETERMINATION important, and what difference does it really make? Think of it this way: Where would you be today if Jesus had not been determined to go to the cross for you? Or if the disciples had not been determined to give their lives for the gospel? Or if your friend, loved one, neighbor, or church had not been determined to share the salvation message with you?

The determination of others has already made a difference in your life. Determination comes from a place of conviction and purpose that what you want to see come to pass is worth fighting for and believing in. In the same way that the determination of others has made space for you, it is time for you to fight and believe in a way that can make the difference for someone else.

SCRIPTURE PASSAGE

As we have already seen, to change is to replace something. We have all had some walls that have burned down, whether from an attack of the enemy or through our own self-sabotage or lack of self-discipline. To change, restore, and rebuild is going to require determination. There is no better guide to this process of restoration than Nehemiah. As you read this story, think about the walls that have burned in your own life that you need the determination to rebuild.

> The words of Nehemiah the son of Hakaliah. In the month Kislev, in the twentieth year, while I was in Susa the palace, Hanani, one of my relatives, and some men of Judah arrived. So I asked them concerning the returning Jews who had been in captivity, and concerning Jerusalem. They said to me, "The remnant that returned from captivity is there in the province enduring great affliction and reproach. Also, the wall of Jerusalem remains broken down, and its gates have been burned with fire."
>
> When I heard these words, I sat down and wept and mourned for days. Then I fasted, and prayed before the God of heaven, and said: "I beseech You, O Lord God of heaven, the great and awesome God, who keeps covenant and mercy for those who love Him and keep His commandments. Let Your ear now be attentive, and Your eyes open, that You may hear the prayer of Your servant, which I now pray before You, day and night, for the children of Israel Your servants, and confess the sins of the children of Israel, which we have sinned against You. Both my father's house and I have sinned. We have acted very corruptly against You and have not obeyed the commandments, nor the statutes, nor the judgments, which You commanded Your servant Moses.
>
> "Please remember the word that You commanded Your servant Moses, saying, 'If you behave unfaithfully, then I will scatter you among the nations, but if you return to Me and keep My commandments and do them, though your outcasts are under the farthest part of the heavens, I will gather them from there and bring them back to the place where I have chosen to establish My name.'"
>
> —NEHEMIAH 1:1–9, MEV

GOING DEEPER

Have you ever wanted something so badly that you would have even given your life for it? Have you ever had a burden or passion or conviction burning in your soul? To know something of that passion, you know something of the story of Nehemiah, a man who loved his God and his city, Jerusalem.

Although Nehemiah had never been to Jerusalem, he'd heard stories of old and found himself in those stories—stories of faith in the God he served. His people had been taken captive long before he was born, and he grew up in Babylon, where he became a cup-bearer to the king.

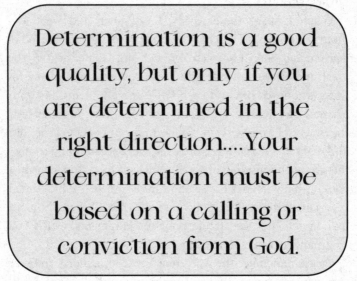

Determination is a good quality, but only if you are determined in the right direction....Your determination must be based on a calling or conviction from God.

As it is for any of us, the life Nehemiah had lived was the only life he knew. But his heart recognized the geography of the great city Jerusalem, his homeland, even though his eyes had never seen it. Finally, he got the report that the city walls had been burned down.

Scripture tells us that when he heard the news, Nehemiah sat down and wept and mourned, fasting and praying before the Lord God of heaven. Everything in his soul was stirring to go to Jerusalem, to lead the charge and rebuild the temple. This was a determined man who would prove to be a leader in Israel.

Nehemiah was a hero. He stood strong against his enemies and against adversity. He had only one goal in mind: to rebuild the house of God.

Often our passions and visions run into obstacles, as it was for Nehemiah, for our enemy is fierce and crafty. But when we are determined, the tactics of the enemy do not dictate the agenda for our lives.

The definition of *determination* is firmness of purpose and resoluteness. Nehemiah was firm in his purpose. He was *resolved* to build the walls of Jerusalem.

Determination is a good quality, but only if you are determined in the right direction. You cannot be focused on pride or power or prestige; your determination must be based on a calling or conviction from God.

In today's culture it's easy to give up on an assignment or project. It is easier to give up than to push through. I recently read an article on LinkedIn that stated that research shows only 8 percent of people achieve their dreams and goals, while 92 percent give up or fail to do so. What is different about the 8 percent? I would say determination.[1]

The beautiful thing about determination is that it activates your faith. When my husband and I first started Influence Church, we started in a school, and then graduated to a theater, but we knew we wanted a home of our own. On my prayer walk one day I passed the Anaheim Hills post office, which had a for sale sign on it. I knew it would be the perfect location for a church. I began to pray and ask God to move in our favor so we could buy the building.

Several weeks after announcing to the church that we wanted to purchase a building, a gentleman approached us saying he would give us the loan. Of course you can imagine how thrilled we were. We signed the paperwork and began planning for our new church building. But as God would have it, He wanted to strengthen our faith—our determination. Just a few weeks before we were to close on the loan, the gentleman let us know he would be unable to fulfill his commitment.

The beautiful thing about broken promises is that they can lead us to prayer and fasting. We called our church to a corporate fast to pray and believe in God. Although our faith was exercised, I must say we were also determined. We filled out more than 130 applications to secure a loan but heard nothing but crickets. Our church board was determined we would not lose our down payment. Once again, the act of determination played a big role in what would happen next.

Someone approached us through a mutual friend and was willing to give us a loan. God had a different plan than we did. His ways are always higher and go beyond our understanding. Just as Nehemiah was determined to build the walls of his city, we were determined to build the walls of our church. God moves through determined people, especially when they activate their faith to see Him move.

FOR FURTHER STUDY

The following scriptures are all invitations to stand firm, to keep fighting, and to withstand temptation. They give us fuel for the road we are traveling. Digest these words prayerfully and allow Holy Spirit to fill you with holy determination to walk your own road to change.

- James 1:12

- 1 Corinthians 16:13

- 2 Chronicles 20:17

- 2 Corinthians 12:10

- Luke 21:19

- 2 Timothy 4:7

COACHING STEPS

1. Your determination cannot come from a place of frustration, only from focus. Sometimes we get angry or put out with a matter and take things into our own hands. This only leads to mistakes and regrets. Before you push through in your own effort, ask God to give you clarity and strength to know how to ascertain the situation. Then with the right attitude, like Nehemiah, be determined to complete the assignment.

2. Not only did Nehemiah have his critics but he also had spies. Often we are called to do something that seems too hard for us to do. People discourage us or use us for their own agenda. Determination in God comes from a place much deeper than our intellect— it comes from our spirit. Make sure you are listening to the right voices speaking into your life.

3. Don't give yourself permission to be lazy. As I mentioned, today's culture is always looking for the easy way out. Determination comes from a place of discipline. If you don't learn to push yourself into new

adventures and experiences, you will never discover all God has for you. Where are you compromising yourself?

THE MOSES FAST

Nehemiah refers to Moses and the law in his prayer to God. He takes responsibility for the sins of his father's house as well as his own. Note that Nehemiah is fasting at the time of his prayer. He, like Moses, was determined to see God move on behalf of the children of Israel.

If you remember the story of Moses on Mount Sinai, you will recall that Moses came down the mountain only to discover that the people were worshipping false gods. In his surprise and anger, Moses threw the Ten Commandments down on the ground and the tablets shattered into a hundred pieces. This was not the way he'd seen the commandments being presented to the people.

Determined to get it right, Moses went back up the mountain for another teaching session with God. This time, God took him even deeper in intimacy. The forty-day fast proved to be a time of great spiritual understanding for Moses. Determination was one of Moses' greatest qualities. It is only with a spirit of determination and honor to God that you will see your assignment come into alignment and fulfillment.

DISCUSSION QUESTIONS

- Today we talked about the determination Nehemiah had to stay focused on his assignment. Do you find yourself giving up or giving in before you see your dream come true? Maybe it's a business idea, a book, or a relationship that needs repair. Have you stopped trying? Are you willing to pick up where you left off? Are you ready to complete the assignment and revive the passion you once had? Determination starts with you. What steps are you willing to take to put your commitment back into motion?

- Today's culture is entitled and even a bit lazy. We have justified our lack of completion because of our circumstances or the behavior of others. But determination comes from a heart of conviction and confidence. Have you bought into today's mindset? If so, how can you make course corrections and follow through with a commitment you have made or a dream you've had?

- Moses made a mistake. He got angry and threw down the very words God had given him for the people. If he had stopped there, the story would be over for him—but he did not. Determination grew within him, and back up the mountain he went. Maybe you have made a mistake and feel like a failure; let me tell you, you are not. God wants you to pick yourself back up and start again. In what area do you need to start over again? God wants to meet you back on top of the mountain.

PRAYER

Dear Lord, today I realized the things I have given up on and the areas I have not been faithful to. Please give me the strength and determination to complete my task and kingdom assignment. I know You have equipped me for so much more, and I want to be faithful to You and those around me. In Jesus' name, amen.

JOURNAL ENTRY

day
03

FASTING FOR
COURAGE

ESTHER

Courage is contagious. When a brave man takes a
stand, the spines of others are often stiffened.

—BILLY GRAHAM

cour·age | ˈkə-rij |

noun

the ability to do something that frightens one

strength in the face of pain or grief

SIGNS OF LACK OF COURAGE

- You find yourself fearful and frozen.
- You cannot make quick decisions.
- You look for someone else to take the lead.
- You make excuses for why you have not finished something.
- You don't take risks.

I CAN'T EVEN IMAGINE how a group of people could want to totally annihilate another group of people, yet this was the story of Esther. She was a young queen when she came into office—quiet, submissive, and beautiful. Her God had put her in the perfect place at the right time to save a nation. Often, courage rises up from within when we face a conflict with conviction.

SCRIPTURE PASSAGES

On this road to change you are going to face resistance. Esther gives us a wonderful account of how even in the face of adversaries, enemies, and conflict we can see God move mightily on our behalf. As you read this story, think about how it relates to your own.

> After these things King Ahasuerus praised Haman the son of Hammedatha the Agagite, and promoted him, and set his seat above all the officials who were with him. All the

king's servants, when they were at the king's gate, bowed or paid homage to Haman since the king had commanded it. Mordecai, however, never bowed or paid homage.

So the king's servants tending the king's gate said to Mordecai, "Why are you transgressing the king's commandment?" Though they spoke to him daily, he never listened to them, so they reported it to Haman to see if the words of Mordecai would stand, for Mordecai had told them that he was a Jew.

When Haman saw that Mordecai neither bowed nor paid him homage, he was filled with rage. But he disdained to lay hands on only Mordecai, since they had told him of the people of Mordecai. So Haman sought to destroy all the Jews throughout the whole kingdom of Ahasuerus.

—ESTHER 3:1–6, MEV

When Mordecai learned all that had been done, he tore his clothes and put on sackcloth with ashes, and went out into the midst of the city, and cried with a loud and bitter cry. He went as far as the king's gate because no one was allowed to enter into the king's gate clothed with sackcloth. In each and every province where the king's command and his decree came there was great mourning among the Jews, and fasting, and weeping, and wailing. Many lay in sackcloth and ashes.

So the young women of Esther and her eunuchs came and told her of it. The queen was then seized by anguish. She sent garments to clothe Mordecai so that he could remove his sackcloth, but he would not accept them. So Esther summoned Hathak, one of the king's eunuchs appointed to attend her, and commanded him concerning Mordecai to learn what this was about and why.

So Hathak went out to where Mordecai was in the area of the city in front of the king's gate. Mordecai told him about all that had happened to him and about the sum of silver that Haman had promised to pay to the king's treasuries for the destruction of the Jews. Mordecai also gave him a copy of the written decree issued in Susa concerning their destruction so he could show Esther, tell her about it, and then charge her to go to the king in order to gain him favor with the king and to make requests in the presence of the king for her people.

Hathak returned and told Esther the words of Mordecai. Again Esther spoke to Hathak and ordered him to reply to Mordecai: "All the king's servants and the people of the king's provinces know that whoever, whether man or woman, wishes to come to the king at the inner court but has not been summoned, there is one law—to put him to death—unless for some reason the king should hold out the golden scepter so that he might live. I, however, have not been summoned to come to the king for these thirty days."

So all the words of Esther were told to Mordecai. Then Mordecai told them to reply to Esther, "Do not think that in the king's palace you will be more likely to escape than all the other Jews. For if you remain silent at this time, protection and deliverance for the Jews will be ordained from some other place, but you and your father's house shall be destroyed. And who knows if you may have attained royal position for such a time as this?"

Then Esther replied, sending back to Mordecai: "Go, gather all the Jews who can be found in Susa, then fast for me. Stop eating and drinking for three days, night or day. I and my young women will fast likewise. Only then would I dare go to the king since it is not allowed by law, and if I perish, I perish."

So Mordecai went away and did exactly as Esther had commanded him.

—ESTHER 4:1–17, MEV

GOING DEEPER

The story of Esther is one of great courage and faith. It all starts with a king, a queen, and an evil villain named Haman. (Some scholars say Haman was responsible for having the prophet Daniel killed.) Haman hated the Jews, mostly because of the pride and arrogance that rose in him during an encounter with Esther's cousin Mordecai.

Mordecai would not comply with or submit to Haman's unrealistic laws. He stood strong for his God and his convictions. Without the king's knowledge, Haman devised a plan to completely wipe out the Jews and have them all killed. Mordecai got wind of the strategy and alerted his cousin Esther of the evil scheme.

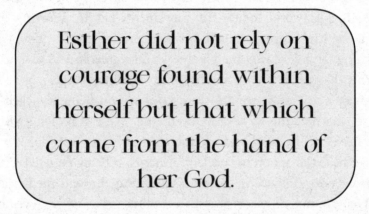

Esther did not rely on courage found within herself but that which came from the hand of her God.

It was God's perfect plan to use Esther in the role of queen to save His people. She had the courage to call the nation to a corporate fast while at the same time creating a strategy to approach the king, which was unthinkable at that time. She believed that God knows the times and seasons, trusting that we are often put in a place of leadership or decision making for such a time as needed.

Esther's courage was strong. Her voice was subtle yet strategic. She did not rely on courage found within herself but that which came from the hand of her God. Some people are more courageous than others, but the courage to stand for a deep conviction can only come from God.

When we ask God for wisdom and insight, He creates a plan no man can destroy. Haman was no competition for the God of Israel. Queen Esther was given a strategy from the hand of God, and the king would soon see the evil devices of his commander, Haman.

We know we are living in uncertain times. I do not remember a time in my life when there has been more pushback and anger against Christians and the local church. More than ever I believe we must be courageous and stand up for our faith and biblical rights as a nation. Proverbs 28:1 says, "The wicked flee when no one pursues, but the righteous are bold as a lion."

My good friend Sean Feucht has been a strong and courageous voice in our world today. His movement, Let Us Worship, has made its way to every state and from shore to shore, worshipping, teaching, and declaring the goodness and righteousness of God. It is time that we all rise up and begin to walk in courage.

Much like Esther, we are seeing our nation being attacked by those who hate the ways of Yahweh God. We can no longer bury our heads in the sand and say there's nothing we can do. We no longer have the option to be silent. America is being targeted. From Broadway to Hollywood, Satan is attacking through media, arts and entertainment, our schools, our politicians—and yes, even our churches. Where are the bold lions? The courageous? Where are those who are ready to change, those who are willing to be educated and become voices for "such a time as this"?

Not only did Esther's courage save her life and the lives of all Jews, but her cousin Mordecai also received promotion and wealth from the very hand of the king—by the end of the story, he is second in command to the king and revered by his people.

When you choose to take a courageous stand for God, get ready for blessings to come your way.

FOR FURTHER STUDY

The following verses will help equip you with the kind of courage we read about in Esther. As you read them, ask God to fill you with this same courage for the battles you are facing now.

- Deuteronomy 31:6
- Joshua 1:9
- 1 Chronicles 28:20
- 1 Corinthians 16:13
- Psalm 27:1
- Psalm 56:3–4
- Isaiah 41:10

COACHING STEPS

1. Everyone has feelings of fear and discouragement at times. Part of growing in your courage is *embracing the need to grow.*

2. It is important to surround yourself with risk-oriented people—those who will challenge you and encourage you to push past your fears or roadblocks. Ask someone you admire to have coffee with you, and then give them permission to hold you accountable to a goal on your bucket list.

3. Get comfortable with being uncomfortable. If you don't embrace discomfort, you will never change. Growth and change take time and discipline. If you

want to become more courageous, you must take risks that make you uncomfortable. You will be glad you did.

THE MOSES FAST

Can you imagine the courage it took for Moses to go up the mountain alone with God? He had seen the power of the all-consuming God firsthand. He had walked step by step through the wilderness, across the deserts, and along the seas with this God. Now he had chosen to go by himself—alone—on a journey with God. The Scriptures tell us Moses fasted for forty days—twice, actually. He fasted for the first set of commandments, and then again for his second round with God. I believe Moses grew in courage through the process.

We are all so consumed with our requests that we often forget God is more consumed with our growth. Courage comes through crisis and conflict—it's how we grow. It's how we mature and see the power of God in our lives. Moses is a great example of how a fearful follower can become a faithful spiritual father. Take courage, my friend; God is working on your behalf.

DISCUSSION QUESTIONS

- It's important to take baby steps to grow your courage. Think of something you have been wanting to try or do—an activity or sport, or even a new career. Now, what is one thing you can do today to start moving in that direction? Write out your action steps.

- I love the story of Queen Esther because she showed so much courage despite her age and circumstances. Her faith makes me want to be bold. Today's culture has become weak. In what ways can you be bold and take a stand for your convictions?

- Today we talked about how hard it was for Moses to walk up the mountain alone with God. Have you ever had a moment alone with God when you felt afraid? God's plan is to meet you on the mountain, to walk and talk with you along the way. Take a few moments and write down your thoughts about the current state of your relationship with God.

PRAYER

Dear Lord, I desire to grow in my courage by taking bold steps in faith. I ask that You bring opportunities that will cause me to trust You with my life. I desire to walk up the mountain with You and experience new levels of spiritual maturity. In Jesus' name, amen.

JOURNAL ENTRY

_____

_____

_____

_____

FASTING FOR
FAITH

DANIEL

Faith sees the invisible, believes the unbelievable,

and receives the impossible.

—CORRIE TEN BOOM

faith | ˈfāth |

noun

belief and trust in and loyalty to God[1]

SIGNS OF LACK OF FAITH

- You quit projects you started.
- You make excuses for not following through.
- You talk more than you work.
- You are easily overwhelmed.
- You lose focus.

FAITH DOES NOT come with age or church membership; faith comes from exercising your ask. It comes from believing God can and does work on your behalf. Faith moves in the unseen realm and manifests in miracles and answered prayer. God is waiting for you to petition Him for your need and request. It just takes faith the size of a mustard seed to move the mountains in your life.

SCRIPTURE PASSAGE

It takes extraordinary faith to experience sweeping change in our lives. There is no better image of the kind of radical trust we are invited into than the story of Daniel. As you read this familiar story, ask where you find yourself in it today.

> But Daniel purposed in his heart that he would not defile himself with the portion of the king's food, nor with the wine which he drank. Therefore he requested of the master of the officials that he might not defile himself. Now God had brought Daniel into favor and compassion with the master of the officials. The master of the officials said to Daniel, "I

fear my lord the king who has appointed your food and your drink. For why should he see your faces worse-looking than the youths who are your age? Then you would endanger my head before the king."

Then Daniel said to the steward, whom the master of the officials had set over Daniel, Hananiah, Mishael, and Azariah, "Please test your servants for ten days, and let them give us vegetables to eat and water to drink. Then let our countenances be looked upon before you, and the countenance of the youths who eat of the portion of the king's food. And as you see, deal with your servants." So he consented to them in this matter and tested them for ten days.

At the end of ten days their countenances appeared fairer and fatter than all the youths who ate the portion of the king's food. Thus the guard continued to take away the portion of their food and the wine that they were to drink, and gave them vegetables. As for these four youths, God gave them knowledge and skill in every branch of learning and wisdom. And Daniel had understanding in all kinds of visions and dreams.

Now at the end of the days that the king had set for them to be brought in, the master of the officials brought them in before Nebuchadnezzar. The king spoke with them, and, among them all, none was found like Daniel, Hananiah, Mishael, and Azariah. Therefore they served before the king. In all matters of wisdom and understanding which the king inquired of them, he found them ten times better than all the magicians and astrologers that were in all his realm. Daniel continued even to the first year of King Cyrus.

—Daniel 1:8–21, mev

GOING DEEPER

Each day we are looking at different characteristics and behaviors that cause us to grow in our walk with Christ. I cannot think of a greater area in which to grow than the area of faith.

Today's fasting focus is one that, if embraced and cultivated, will change everything about your future. The prophet Daniel was a true man of faith. Whether he was in the lion's den, confronting the king's orders, revealing prophecies, or exercising faith through a fast, this man truly walked with God.

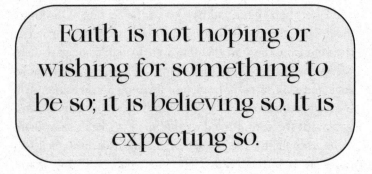

Faith is not hoping or wishing for something to be so; it is believing so. It is expecting so.

It took faith for Daniel, at the age of seventeen, to approach the king's steward and request to be tested and not eat the food from the king's table. It took faith to fast from the delicacies and wine that the king offered and eat only vegetables and drink only water, seeking his God for wisdom and revelation rather than the king's favor. It took faith to challenge the king's steward that if after ten days Daniel was not healthier than the king's men, the steward could do with him as he pleased.

The Bible tells us in Daniel 1:17, "As for these four young men, God gave them knowledge and skill in all literature and wisdom; and Daniel had understanding in all visions and dreams."

Daniel was a man of conviction and faith in his God, and the king's servants hated him for it. Looking for any reason to frame and convict him, they presented the king with a plan that no one could bend the knee to any king but Darius for thirty days. Anyone who violated this order would be thrown into the lion's den if found guilty. Daniel knew he could not compromise with his God. As was his habit, he went into his upper room with his windows opened toward Jerusalem and knelt down three times that day, praying and giving thanks to his God.

"Got you!" The king's men conspired, but the God of Daniel was not finished with His faithful servant.

When you fast and pray and yield your life to God, others are watching. King Darius loved Daniel and saw a man of faith who was loyal to his God. Yet even with the king's favor, being true to his vow to God still brought consequences for Daniel—the king had given his own word, so he had no choice but to deliver Daniel over to the lion's den. The king was tormented by his decision. The night Daniel was put into the lion's den, Darius agonized, sleepless and distraught, tossing and turning.

Early the next morning, King Darius rushed to the lion's den to discover the fate of this young man he'd come to have such affection for. Even though he was not yet fully convinced that Daniel's God was real, he was so compelled by the fierce counter-witness of Daniel and his three friends that he could not help but hope, somewhere deep within—could Daniel's God somehow have preserved him? Could it be?

The king's voice must have cracked as he desperately called out to Daniel, not knowing if he was dead or alive. He was startled to hear the voice of Daniel call back to him, as full of life as ever: "O king, live forever! My God has sent His angel and has shut the lions' mouths so that they have not hurt me, because innocence was found in me before Him; and also before you, O king, I have done no harm" (Dan. 6:21–22, MEV). When Daniel honored God over the applause of other men, God preserved him—and God will preserve you!

This kind of faith is available to us all—but no one is born with it. Walking in faith is a spiritual decision, like that of salvation. You must receive it; you must believe it. You must act it out as though you are already walking in the reality of what you are believing God for. Your faith can be placed only in God, no one else. If you are looking for any other way to exercise faith than in the true God, you will be sorely disappointed. Faith is not hoping or wishing for something to be so; it is believing so. It is expecting so.

"So, how do I become a person of faith?" you might ask. Here is an exercise: Write down something you are asking God for right now. Be as specific as you can—the health of a loved one, the healing of a marriage, financial freedom, personal peace, or whatever need is pressing on you today.

Now, look at that prayer request. Do you see God working on your behalf in this situation? Below the prayer request, write out exactly how it will look when it's answered: the loved one healthy and healed, the restored marriage, the wayward child home safely, your financial resources overflowing in abundance—the exact picture of what you were praying for. Now, look at it. See it. Decree and declare it. Walk in it as though it is your reality.

That is what exercising faith looks like. You see your answer coming each and every day. You are not defined by the negative circumstances you are currently living in but by the future reality of your faith. That's how Daniel lived. He did not see himself going into the lion's den; he saw himself coming out. He did not see himself failing in his fast; he saw himself victorious. He did not see his current situation; he saw the prophecies God gave him becoming reality. Faith is saying it is so and walking into that reality with God.

I have had many faith encounters with God, many prayer requests that became reality simply by taking God at His word and walking in my faith. But not all my requests are seen immediately. There is something I have been asking God for, for over two years now. Although I have not fully seen it yet, I know it's on the way because that is what faith is: believing God through the wait. I am sure that on several occasions Daniel wondered when God would show up and come through on his behalf, but he continued to wait. That's where we find faith; that's where we find God—believing while we wait. Faith is produced in the recesses, through the quiet hours of the soul.

FOR FURTHER STUDY

The following verses call you to wait, to endure, to trust, to keep going. Spend some time in the quiet hours rehearsing these promises of God until you feel your own faith begin to rise.

- Philippians 4:13
- 2 Timothy 4:7
- Jeremiah 29:11
- Romans 15:4
- Hebrews 12:1

COACHING STEPS

1. Mentorship and discipleship are key components of spiritual maturity. Identify someone you know who has strong faith. Ask them to share their story of how

they grew on their journey of faith. Ask questions
and take notes.

2. Create a list of five to ten Bible verses on faith. Now,
ask Holy Spirit to teach you what each verse means
and to take you deeper on the journey to understanding and growing your faith.

3. Go on a prayer walk. I am a big believer in prayer
walking—something about motion and praying
seems to open my understanding and helps me hear
from God on a deeper level. It takes time to develop
your conversation with God—but don't give up. Make
a commitment to walk far enough that you can't
get home quickly. This makes more time for you to
talk with God. While you are walking, ask God to
teach you about faith. Talk with Him about a need or
request that you have, and then press in to exercise
your faith to see it become reality.

THE MOSES FAST

Moses was a man of faith. How else could he have witnessed the
mighty acts of God that he did? Managing twelve tribes of Israel
could not have been easy—not to mention leading thousands of
people through a dry wilderness. God would speak to Moses about
what He planned to do, and then Moses had to trust and believe
that God would be true to His word. Moses had to live a life of faith.
I can only imagine the self-talk that he must have engaged in: "Am
I hearing this correctly? Is God really saying this?"

God likes to be found in the questioning. That is where our faith
grows—in the wonder, and in the waiting. Let me encourage you on
your fast today to ask God a few questions. This is how we build

dialogue and relationships. Don't be afraid to ask Him whatever is really on your mind—that is what this fast is for! God wants to hear from you.

DISCUSSION QUESTIONS

- Faith is seeing God move despite what we think or feel; it's seeing God move from the unseen to the seen realm. What is something you are asking God for in your life right now? Exercise your faith now by writing down exactly what you are believing God for.

- Daniel had to exercise his faith time and time again. That is how our faith grows, by building on one faith experience upon another. Your life is to be a journey of faith stories. Take a moment now and write down two or three testimonies that you have had in your life. Start to build a faith library along your life journey.

- Faith does not come merely because you are a Christian. You must discipline yourself to grow in your faith. Like fitness, weight management, or Scripture memorization, you must want it more than you don't. What are some ways you can grow your faith? Make a list of two or three things you can do to stretch and grow your faith.

PRAYER

Dear Lord, I want to grow in my faith. I want to see You move in my life and use me for Your kingdom. I ask that You teach me how to build my faith and walk in the supernatural realm. I want others to witness the testimony of faith from my life and be encouraged to trust in Your plan. In Jesus' name, amen.

JOURNAL ENTRY

_____

_____

_____

_____

_____

_____

_____

_____

_____

day
05

FASTING FOR CONTENTMENT

AARON

Real contentment must come from within. You and I cannot change or control the world around us, but we can change and control the world within us.

—WARREN WIERSBE

con·tent·ment | kən-ˈtent-mənt |

noun

a state of happiness and satisfaction

SIGNS OF LACK OF CONTENTMENT

- You're never satisfied with life.
- You're always chasing a new idea.
- You're never fully happy.
- You're restless and bored.
- You complain about others.

CONTENTMENT IS VISIBLE and can be seen on a person's face. There is a kind of peace and serenity about some people that is contagious. They are at rest with themselves, and it is evident. I think this is how Jesus lived His life—that is why so many people followed Him. Not only did He have the words of life, but He also walked in a calm and approachable manner. Contentment is something we must all long for and pursue.

SCRIPTURE PASSAGES

In the relationship Aaron had with his brother, Moses, we see a beautiful model of contentment. Though Moses was not a naturally gifted orator like his brother, he was called to lead—and Aaron, rather than being jealous or insecure, fully embraced his role. Both of them understood their assignments. As you read this story, think about the roles that have been given to you, and reflect on whether you are choosing contentment or this is an area in which you need to grow.

Then Moses said to the LORD, "O my Lord, I am not eloquent, neither before nor since You have spoken to Your servant. But I am slow of speech, and of a slow tongue."

The LORD said to him, "Who has made man's mouth? Or who made the dumb, or deaf, or the seeing, or the blind? Have not I, the LORD? Now therefore go, and I will be with your mouth and teach you what you must say."

He said, "O my Lord, send, I pray, by the hand of whomever else You will send."

The anger of the LORD was inflamed against Moses, and He said, "Is not Aaron the Levite your brother? I know that he can speak well. And also, he comes out to meet you, and when he sees you, he will be glad in his heart. You shall speak to him and put the words in his mouth, and I will be with your mouth, and with his mouth, and will teach you what you must do. What's more, he will be your spokesman to the people, and he will be as a mouth for you, and you will be as God to him.

—EXODUS 4:10–16, MEV

So the LORD said to Moses, "See, I have made you a god to Pharaoh, and Aaron your brother will be your prophet. You shall speak all that I command you, and Aaron your brother shall tell Pharaoh to send the children of Israel out of his land. But I will harden Pharaoh's heart and multiply My signs and My wonders in the land of Egypt. Nevertheless, Pharaoh will not listen to you, so that I may lay My hand upon Egypt and bring forth My armies and My people, the children of Israel, out of the land of Egypt by great judgments. And the Egyptians shall know that I am the LORD when I stretch forth My hand upon Egypt and bring out the children of Israel from among them." So Moses and Aaron did it. Just as the LORD commanded them, so they did.

—EXODUS 7:1–6, MEV

GOING DEEPER

Do you have siblings, cousins, or even close friends? If so, you don't need me to tell you that rivalry and jealousy are a natural part of humanity. Something about competition or favoritism just brings out a spirit of comparison. That's why I love the story of Aaron and his little brother, Moses—it is a stark and beautiful contrast to the way we often experience these kinds of familial relationships. Most of us know how God used Moses to lead the children of Israel out of captivity, but you may not know how important it was that his brother was by his side.

Moses had two older siblings, a brother named Aaron and a sister named Miriam. Although they did not take center stage, they were a vital part of the journey of the Israelites.

We saw how God chose Moses to be His spokesman, His mouthpiece, His author, and that Moses rejected the offer by responding that he did not have the ability to speak and stuttered and stammered when he tried to talk. But God had a plan; God always has a plan. When God told Moses that He would use his brother, Aaron, to speak for him, Moses felt a sense of comfort in his assignment.

Although Moses envisioned Aaron being his mouthpiece, once he stepped into God's calling for his life, Moses could not stop talking. Aaron did not have many opportunities to speak because Moses found confidence in his God-given ability. It was his destiny.

What we do find in Aaron, however, is contentment. He was content to walk alongside and encourage his brother to submit to the authority of God's leader. He was content to use his gifts and talents as a high priest and to speak to the people on behalf of God's law without trying to compete with his brother.

Contentment is a state in which our souls find rest—where we don't feel the need to outshine, outtalk, or outperform any other person. There is a sense of rest in our being that finds peace and serenity.

You know you are content when you continue to pursue your interests and passions and abilities without comparing or competing with others. Competition and contentment are polar opposites.

Aaron chose to wait on Moses' leadership as they approached Pharaoh, as he did when they walked up Mount Sinai, and again when they crossed the Red Sea, and all along the way walking through the wilderness. Leadership comes in different forms and different positions. We must strive to be content in the areas of leadership to which God has assigned us.

My husband and I have pastored churches for many years. Although we are both entrepreneurs and leaders in our own right, it is all too easy to compare ourselves with other ministries and churches. It's so easy to embrace the spirit of competition in all places and stages of life, even in ministry. When we hear about a church, company, or organization doing something innovative or impactful, we whisper to others, "Ooh, that's nothing new; we have done that before." Or we look for the flaws and failures in the program to justify our own lack of creativity or effort.

> Aaron did not take on the spirit of competition with his little brother. He was content with his God-given assignment to aid and assist.

We all tend to want to be bigger and better than those around us. At times our desire for success leads us to push ourselves beyond what God has planned for us—all in the spirit of competition.

I desire contentment in my spirit. How about you? Don't get me wrong. I am not talking about laziness or apathy but about the peace and rest that come when we are doing our best and simply running in our own lane with God.

Aaron did not take on the spirit of competition with his little brother. He was content with his God-given assignment to aid and assist. To be fair, there were a few times when Aaron ran ahead of Moses and took matters into his own hands, but when confronted with the truth he repented and stepped right back into his role as encourager and confidant to Moses.

The truth is that we all experience times of jealousy and compare ourselves with others. Those moments come, but the goal is to know your role and purpose on this earth, and to encourage those God puts in your path along the way. Be content with who you are and what you have to offer to humanity.

FOR FURTHER STUDY

The following passages illuminate the way of contentment. Read them prayerfully, allowing yourself to let go of any competition, strife, or jealousy. Let these words draw you into a place of rest and trust.

- Philippians 4:11–13
- 1 Timothy 6:6–12
- 2 Corinthians 12:9–10
- Romans 8:28

- Job 36:11
- Proverbs 19:23

COACHING STEPS

1. Identify the things you do well. Now ask yourself, "Am I doing my best in each of these areas?"
   Contentment comes from within by not comparing
   yourself to others, but it also means you are achieving
   your personal best.

2. Ask yourself if there is anyone of whom you are
   envious or jealous. If so, ask yourself why. You will
   never find complete contentment until you are completely at peace with who you are.

3. Being challenged and encouraged to grow is a good
   thing. Never stop learning and becoming better at
   your skill—but never try to impersonate someone
   else. Personal contentment is a two-edged sword: One
   side is complete rest with peace and joy. The other
   side is the desire to work hard at honing your gifts
   and skills to be your personal best self.

THE MOSES FAST

I believe fasting takes us deeper with God. It is a spiritual discipline
that causes us to rely completely on Him. When our flesh cries out
to be fed, fasting reminds us we are waiting on God for something
bigger than we can find in ourselves.

A sense of contentment is found in the process of trusting

God for your breakthrough. God has His own timetable, and He knows exactly when to come through. Contentment says, "I trust You, Lord, to work and act on my behalf." Although we read about many times Moses questioned and even disobeyed God along the journey, he always turned back to believing and trusting that God loved him and had a plan for his life. That is what contentment is: trusting God and resting in His will and destiny for your life.

DISCUSSION QUESTIONS

- Working with family can be challenging at times. How is your relationship with your family? As we have witnessed, the pandemic brought out a lot of family dissension and conflict. Is there someone you need to ask for forgiveness, or a situation for which you need to make restitution?

- Aaron had to be willing to step aside from his little brother, Moses, to see God use him in extraordinary ways. Jealousy is a natural emotional response when we feel overlooked or unseen. Is there anything in your life that you need to confess and release to God? Embracing our God-given talents and assignments is the first step to having complete peace and lives free of comparison.

- Are you happy? I mean, are you content with the gifts and talents God has given you? Sometimes we find ourselves stuck in life because we are living vicariously through the story of someone else. True contentment comes when we know how God has gifted us and we flow in our unique ability to be who God created us to be. What would you say are your gifts, abilities, and ministry? Are you using them for the kingdom of God?

PRAYER

Dear Lord, I confess I am not always content with my life. I ask that You show me how to trust and rely on Your plans for my journey. Help me to develop my God-given talents for Your kingdom and my calling. I ask for a spirit of peace and contentment to be part of my life every day. Take from me the temptation to be jealous or to compare myself with others. In Jesus' name, amen.

JOURNAL ENTRY

_____

_____

_____

_____

_____

_____

_____

day
06

FASTING FOR
LEADERSHIP

JOSHUA

A man who wants to lead the orchestra must

turn his back on the crowd.

—MAX LUCADO

lead·er·ship | ˈlē-dər-ˌship |

noun

the action of leading a group of people or an organization

the state or position of being a leader

SIGNS OF LACK OF LEADERSHIP

- You look for someone else to take the lead.
- You make excuses for not helping.
- You find fault with the process.
- You lack drive and confidence.
- You think about the past more than the future.

THE WAY TO identify a leader is to look for someone who surrounds themselves with other leaders—someone who is strong, courageous, eager to learn, and who does not make excuses This is the kind of leader we find in the story of Joshua, the man who followed in the footsteps of Moses and brought the children of Israel into the Promised Land. He was not Moses—he was Joshua. His leadership approach was different, yet perfect for the moment.

God had been preparing Joshua for his next assignment. In Numbers 14:6–10, Moses sent out twelve spies to check out the land, and ten came back with a bad report and only two with a good report. Joshua was one who brought back a good report. He saw the possibility, not the problem—that is a leadership mindset.

SCRIPTURE PASSAGE

As we continue to reflect on character as we fast, Joshua gives us a template for the kind of leaders we can and must become. As you read his story, note what is distinctive about Joshua's own approach to leadership, and reflect on how you might apply these principles in your own life.

Now after the death of Moses the servant of the LORD, the LORD spoke to Joshua son of Nun, the assistant of Moses: "Moses My servant is dead, so now get up and cross over the Jordan—you and all this people—to the land that I am giving to the children of Israel. I have given you every place that the sole of your foot shall tread, as I said to Moses. From the wilderness and this Lebanon, as far as the great river, the River Euphrates, all the land of the Hittites, and to the Mediterranean Sea toward the setting of the sun will be your territory. No man will be able to stand against you all the days of your life. As I was with Moses, I will be with you. I will not abandon you. I will not leave you.

"Be strong and courageous, for you shall provide the land that I swore to their fathers to give them as an inheritance for this people. Be strong and very courageous, in order to act carefully in accordance with all the law that My servant Moses commanded you. Do not turn aside from it to the right or the left, so that you may succeed wherever you go. This Book of the Law must not depart from your mouth. Meditate on it day and night so that you may act carefully according to all that is written in it. For then you will make your way successful, and you will be wise. Have not I commanded you? Be strong and courageous. Do not be afraid or dismayed, for the LORD your God is with you wherever you go."

Then Joshua commanded the officers of the people, "Pass through the midst of the camp and command the people, 'Prepare food, for in three days you will cross the Jordan to go to take possession of the land that the LORD your God is giving you to possess.'"

To the Reubenites, the Gadites, and to the half-tribe of Manasseh, Joshua said, "Remember the word that Moses the servant of the LORD commanded you: 'The LORD your God has given you a place for rest and will give this land.' Your wives, your children, and your livestock may live in the land that Moses gave you on the east side of the Jordan. But you must cross over with your brothers fully armed, your mighty men of valor, and help them, until the LORD has given your brothers rest, as He has given you, and they also have possessed the land that the LORD your God is giving to them. Then you may return to your own land and possess what Moses the servant of the LORD gave you on the east side of the Jordan where the sun rises."

They answered Joshua, "All that you command us we will do, and wherever you send us we will go. Just as we obeyed Moses in all things, we will obey you. May the LORD your God be with you, as He was with Moses!"

—JOSHUA 1:1–17, MEV

GOING DEEPER

Some people are born with a leadership mentality, and others are taught. Joshua was a faithful aide to Moses. Sitting under his discipleship and authority, Joshua learned what it took to be a leader.

Joshua was hungry for God and for the anointing that comes on leaders who chase after His will. He witnessed firsthand the relationship God had with his servant Moses, and he longed to have this kind of intimacy. In Exodus 33:11 we read these words: "So the LORD spoke to Moses face to face, as a man speaks to his friend. And he would return to the camp, but his servant Joshua the son of Nun, a young man, did not depart from the tabernacle."

Leadership is attractive, and many people desire to be in charge. But a true leader is humble and ready to hear from God and to meet Him face to face.

I can only imagine how intimidated Joshua must have felt when Moses handed off the mantle to him. This was Moses the magnificent—the one who parted the Red Sea, met God in a burning bush, and journeyed up Mount Sinai to receive the Ten Commandments. It is easy to feel intimidated by strong leaders. But when God puts a calling on your life, you must be obedient. The insecurities and fears are real, but once you start walking forward in your assignment, your confidence will grow. Joshua had no idea of all that God would do through him, beginning with bringing down the walls of Jericho.

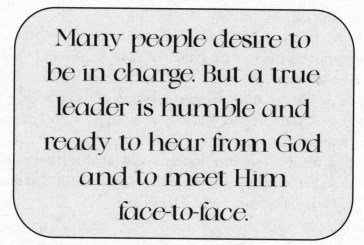

> Many people desire to be in charge. But a true leader is humble and ready to hear from God and to meet Him face-to-face.

As we saw yesterday, there is no place for competition in leadership. Leadership is an individual calling for a specific assignment.

Joshua was a different kind of leader than Moses, and the Israelites soon saw their divergence in leadership styles.

God gave Joshua a strategy to lead his people into the Promised Land. From the spies who scoped out Jericho to the brilliant execution of walking into Canaan, this was now on Joshua's watch. Moses had disobeyed God and, therefore, would not see the fulfillment of his assignment. The torch was now passed to Joshua. He would lead Israel not only into the Promised Land but also into their future.

Leaders need wisdom and strategy along with humility. This was not about Joshua—this was about the fulfillment of a promise God gave to His people. One of the many lessons we learn from this story is that we have an opportunity and responsibility to partner with God in our assignments. There is always room for forgiveness and course correction when we disobey God, but there are also consequences for our choices.

Joshua had learned a lot from the way Moses followed God through his own highs and lows, but now it was time for him to learn from God.

The Book of Joshua is a testimony to the next generations on their journey to conquer the Promised Land. The reign of Joshua lasted about twenty-five years after the death of Moses. It would take seven years to finally possess the land of Canaan. Over the next several years, Joshua would lead Israel to victory through many military campaigns.

Almost twenty years later, Joshua would address the nation for his final exhortation, a testimony to the faithfulness of God during all those years of his own faithful leadership.

FOR FURTHER STUDY

Prayerfully reflect on the following scriptures that take us further into understanding the kind of leaders God wants us to be, the kind of leadership we are asking God to cultivate within us during our fast.

- Proverbs 22:29
- 1 Timothy 3:13
- 1 Timothy 4:12
- 2 Timothy 2:15

- Psalm 78:72

- Acts 20:28

COACHING STEPS

1. One of the primary things you can do as a leader is build healthy relationships—not only for networking opportunities, but more importantly, for account- ability. Good leaders are always learning and growing in their knowledge as well as their well-being. Holding yourself accountable to others is like placing a safety net all around in case you fall.

2. Wise leaders develop people. It is critically important that you are always building other leaders around you. You will never grow until you find someone to replace you in your position. You must fill the void of where you currently are to rotate to a higher level. Are you developing others right now? If not, whom might God be calling you to develop?

3. Good leaders communicate clearly. They are precise and to the point; they don't overtalk. Leaders do not try to be everyone's friend. They make decisions that will impact the future, and their first focus is leading well. They speak with authority and confidence. How are you practicing this discipline in your life? What would it look like for you to practice more concise, clear communication?

THE MOSES FAST

I love today's quote: "A man who wants to lead the orchestra must turn his back on the crowd." This was exactly where Moses found himself. His back was to the children of Israel, but he was face to face with God. Leadership is lonely at times, often even difficult. But when you have been called by God, you have no other joy.

As Moses stayed committed to his forty-day fast, God gave him clarity to lead the people. His wisdom in leadership was a direct download from heaven. When you are focused solely on the face of God, you will have insight, wisdom, and revelation from the hand of God. Fasting opens doors to the eternal realm.

DISCUSSION QUESTIONS

- Have you ever been in the shadow of a powerful leader? How did you discover your own leadership qualities? What is your strongest leadership skill?

- Joshua had to be still and listen to the word coming from God before he could step into his new leadership role. I am sure he questioned his assignment from time to time. Have you ever struggled with something God has asked you to do? Are you willing to accept the assignment God has aligned for you? Leadership begins by saying yes to God.

- Smart leaders build accountability into their lives. Friends, family, and colleagues can all be great resources to make you a healthier leader, while the Word of God and spiritual leaders can keep you grounded. Whom do you have in your life to hold you accountable? Have you been honest and vulnerable with them? If you don't have those people in your life right now, who might you ask?

PRAYER

Dear Lord, I believe You have equipped me to be a leader in my sphere of influence. Help me to stand strong for my conviction and lead others to embrace their God-given talents. I ask that You give me the wisdom I need to fulfill my destiny and be all You have created me to be. In Jesus' name, amen.

JOURNAL ENTRY

_____

_____

_____

_____

_____

_____

_____

day
07

FASTING FOR
LOYALTY

RUTH

One can believe in the divinity of Jesus Christ and feel no personal loyalty to Him at all—indeed, pay no attention whatever to His commandments and His will for one's life. One can believe intellectually in the efficacy of prayer and never do any praying.

—MAX LUCADO

loy·al·ty | ˈlȯi(-ə)l-tē |

noun

a strong feeling of support or allegiance[1]

SIGNS OF LACK OF LOYALTY

- You are defensive when asked questions.
- You don't want to share information.
- You do not like to make a commitment.
- You are not interested in others.
- You are always looking for a better opportunity.

Loyalty is a characteristic that is not often talked about in today's culture. We are more interested in entitlement or personal choices than in the value of relationships. But what would it look like if we shifted back to the core values of humanity—putting others first, being people of our word, and respecting the commitments we have made? I think it might look like the story we will read from Scripture today about a young woman who was loyal to the vow she had made.

SCRIPTURE PASSAGE

As you read today's passage, pay special attention to the virtue of loyalty you see on display here. How might God want to use this time of fasting to take you into deeper fidelity in your walk with Him?

> So she got up with her daughters-in-law to return from the land of Moab, for in the land of Moab, she had heard that the LORD had visited His people by giving them food. She set out from

the place where she had been, with her two daughters-in-law, and they went on their way to return to the land of Judah.

Then Naomi said to her two daughters-in-law, "Go, return each to her mother's house. May the LORD deal kindly with you, as you have dealt with your deceased husbands and with me. May the LORD grant that you each find rest in the house of another husband." Then she kissed them, and they raised their voices and wept aloud. They said to her, "We will return with you to your people."

But Naomi said, "Turn back, my daughters. Why would you go with me? Are there sons in my womb, who could become your husbands? Turn back, my daughters! Go, for I am too old to have a husband. Even if I thought that there was still hope for me, that I could have a husband tonight and give birth to sons, would you wait until they were grown? Would you refrain from getting married? No, my daughters. It is much more bitter for me than for you, for the hand of the LORD has turned against me." Then they raised their voices and wept aloud once more. Orpah kissed her mother-in-law, but Ruth clung to her.

Naomi said, "Look, your sister-in-law has returned to her people and her gods. Return with her!"

But Ruth said, "Do not urge me to leave you or to turn back from following you. For wherever you go, I will go, and wherever you stay, I will stay. Your people shall be my people and your God my God. Where you die, I will die, and there I will be buried. May the LORD do thus to me, and worse, if anything but death separates you and me!" When Naomi saw that she was determined to go with her, she said no more to her.

So they both went on until they came to Bethlehem. When they came to Bethlehem, the whole town was stirred because of them, and the women asked, "Is this Naomi?" But she said to them, "Do not call me Naomi. Call me Mara, because the Almighty has brought great bitterness to me. I was full when I left, but the LORD has caused me to return empty. Why should you call me Naomi when the LORD has opposed me? The Almighty has brought misfortune upon me!"

So Naomi returned from the land of Moab with Ruth the Moabite, her daughter-in-law. They came to Bethlehem at the start of the spring barley harvest.

—RUTH 1:6–22, MEV

GOING DEEPER

If you have ever been to a wedding, I'm sure you have heard the minister recite this passage from Ruth chapter 1:

> Entreat me not to leave you, or to turn back from following after you; for wherever you go, I will go; and wherever you lodge, I will lodge; your people shall be my people, and your God, my God.
>
> —RUTH 1:16

Although this is a beautiful verse for couples to use to make a vow and commitment to one another, it was not the context of the passage. This was a comment and commitment Ruth was making to her mother-in-law. A young foreign woman observed the devotion and loyalty her mother-in-law had toward her God.

Ruth kept her commitment. She was loyal to her mother-in-law—and as Ruth's story shows, God blesses loyalty.

Naomi, a woman who is often scorned for her complaining and depressive comments, was also a woman who knew her God. There was a famine in the land of Bethlehem, so Naomi, her husband, and her two sons moved to the country of Moab to survive. Shortly after arriving, her husband, Elimelech, died. Then her sons, Mahlon and Chilion, took wives from the land of Moab. Both women honored and loved their mother-in-law, but the true test of loyalty was soon to be revealed.

After about ten years, both of Naomi's sons died, leaving her widowed with two daughters-in-law. Feeling destitute and quite alone, Naomi decided to make her way back to her homeland, encouraging her daughters-in-law to go back to their father's home. But Ruth would not depart. That's where we pick up the story, with this famous expression of loyalty and commitment.

Ruth was saying that she wanted to be like her mother-in-law. Even in the midst of a crisis there was something deep down in Naomi that Ruth was attracted to. Ruth's being willing to embrace someone else's faith, heritage, and homeland tells us a lot about the love Naomi had for her people and for her God.

In our competitive society it is each person for himself or herself—my ideas, my discovery, my way. It's estimated that the average person changes jobs or careers six times in their lifetime. We live in a culture of so many opportunities! I have heard many stories of people who have taken ideas, concepts, and even business strategies from one company to another just to make a name for themselves.

We can all justify why we do something. We convince ourselves with self-talk like, "I was always overlooked; they didn't see my gifts and talents. I will go where I am appreciated and valued," or, "They did it to me first; I'll have the last laugh. I must be responsible for who I am and my gifts and talents," all while watching the qualities of honor and integrity fly out the window.

But this young woman understood loyalty. Ruth had made a

commitment when she married Naomi's son, and she valued her vow to stay the course. In the culture of that day, when you married a man, you were to embrace the whole family you were marrying into. And although Naomi gave each of the daughters-in-law the opportunity to return, Ruth kept her commitment. She was loyal to her mother-in-law—and as we will see, God blesses loyalty.

As we continue reading the story, we find that when they arrived in Bethlehem, Ruth asked that Naomi allow her to go and glean in the fields after the reapers. This was collecting leftovers, the wheat that no one else wanted—but Ruth did it day after day with a joyful heart.

Did you know that God's timing is perfect? For at the right moment, Boaz, the wealthy landowner who was also a relative of Naomi, was walking among the wheat fields when his eyes fell upon Ruth. Divine destiny was getting ready to play its hand, for Ruth and Boaz would soon fall in love and marry. Because of her loyalty, Ruth would receive one of the greatest blessings of life—she would have a son and name him Obed, who would be in the direct lineage of Jesus Himself.

The story ends with Naomi holding her grandson. God will bless loyalty every time. Let me encourage you now: if you feel that you have been misused or disrespected, remember that God sees it all. He blesses and opens doors of opportunity to those who walk in righteousness and obedience.

FOR FURTHER STUDY

As you prayerfully reflect on these scriptures, ask Holy Spirit to embed within you the kind of loyalty that you read about here, that it would infuse all your relationships, from your relationship with God to your relationships with family and friends.

- Proverbs 18:24

- Proverbs 17:17

- Matthew 26:35

- Proverbs 21:21

- Matthew 18:15

- 1 Corinthians 13:4–7

- 1 Corinthians 4:2

- 1 John 3:24

COACHING STEPS

1. One of the most obvious qualities of a loyal person is that they will stand by you through thick and thin. That does not mean they will always agree with your decisions, but it does mean they are there to give you guidance and direction. A loyal person does not retreat when things get hard. Take a look at your closest relationships and ask yourself, "Am I a loyal friend?"

2. A person who is loyal can celebrate the success of others. They are not jealous or envious but encouraging and genuinely happy for others. When you are with a loyal person, you are free to be yourself without fear of being judged or condemned. How do you measure up to this evaluation? Is there anyone you need to ask to forgive you?

3. Accountability is key to growing as a person. One of the smartest things you can do is to put people

in your life who will be honest and encouraging to you—friends who will stand by you and correct you. Warning: not everyone who is a friend will be loyal to you. Create a list of the qualities you look for in a loyal friend. Using that list as a reference, vet your friendships. If they don't pass the test, be wise about how much you share with them.

THE MOSES FAST

As we learned earlier in our study, Aaron was a loyal brother to Moses. He could be trusted and relied on in times of doubt and fear. Loyal friends and family helped see Moses through his assignment.

Fasting can bring clarity and focus to many areas of our lives, including our relationships. This would be a great time to evaluate your associates as well as your friendships and ask yourself some honest questions: Do you have a network of loyal friends? Have you been a loyal friend yourself? Take time to examine your heart today. God is doing a fresh work in you. "A man who has friends must himself be friendly, but there is a friend who sticks closer than a brother" (Prov. 18:24).

DISCUSSION QUESTIONS

- Ruth did not allow the difficulty of relocation or hard work to stop her from keeping her vow. Do you have that kind of loyalty to friends or family? Share what you think about Ruth leaving her family, friends, and culture to follow Naomi. Would you have done that?

- God blessed Ruth with a son in the direct lineage of Jesus. Do you think it was a result of her obedience, or just being at the right place at the right time? The answer to that question might explain why you have not seen your breakthrough yet. There is no coincidence with God. There are blessings and favor. Share a time God came through for you because of your obedience.

- Moses surrounded himself with loyal companions: Aaron, Hur, Joshua, and many others. Take a moment to think of your most loyal friends, and name them below. Now, take a moment and thank them for their friendship and loyalty. Often we take those we love the most for granted.

PRAYER

Dear Lord, today we discussed loyalty. I want to be a faithful and honest friend to others. God, teach me to put my needs aside and to be present for those I love. Help me to empty myself of any pride that would block my heart and deeds to others. Help me to support those I care about. In Jesus' name, amen.

JOURNAL ENTRY

_____

_____

_____

_____

_____

_____

_____

_____

_____

_____

_____

_____

_____

_____

_____

_____

week two

FASTING WITH ELIJAH

Eᴌɪᴊᴀʜ ᴛʜᴇ ᴘʀᴏᴘʜᴇᴛ hit an emotional and spiritual wall after experiencing a great victory, and then God led him to fast in order to prepare him for what would come next. This fast, for you, is a time of rest, reflection, and preparation for what's ahead. Where do you find yourself in today's passage? Do you feel something of the fatigue, anxiety, depression, or worry that you see in Elijah? Be alert to the ways God may want to use this time to restore you in the areas in which you find yourself depleted.

SCRIPTURE PASSAGE

And Ahab told Jezebel all that Elijah had done and how he had executed all the prophets with the sword. Then Jezebel sent a messenger to Elijah, saying, "So let the gods do to me and more also, if I do not make your life as the life of one of them by tomorrow about this time." When he saw that she was serious, he arose and ran for his life to Beersheba, which belongs to Judah, and left his servant there. But he went a day's journey into the wilderness and came and sat down under a juniper tree and asked that he might die, saying, "It is enough! Now, O Lᴏʀᴅ, take my life, for I am not better than my fathers."

As he lay and slept under the juniper tree, an angel touched him and said to him, "Arise and eat." He looked, and there was a cake baked on coals and a jar of water at his head. And he ate and drank and then lay down again.

The angel of the LORD came again a second time and touched him and said, "Arise and eat, because the journey is too great for you." He arose and ate and drank and went in the strength of that food forty days and forty nights to Horeb, the mountain of God.

He came to a cave and camped there, and the word of the LORD came to him, and He said to him, "Why are you here, Elijah?"

And he said, "I have been very zealous for the LORD, Lord of Hosts, for the children of Israel have forsaken Your covenant, thrown down Your altars, and killed Your prophets with the sword, and I alone am left, and they seek to take my life."

He said, "Go and stand on the mountain before the LORD."

And, behold, the LORD passed by, and a great and strong wind split the mountains and broke in pieces the rocks before the LORD, but the LORD was not in the wind. And after the wind, an earthquake came, but the LORD was not in the earthquake. And after the earthquake, a fire came, but the LORD was not in the fire, and after the fire, a still, small voice. When Elijah heard it, he wrapped his face in his cloak and went out and stood in the entrance to the cave.

And a voice came to him and said, "Why are you here, Elijah?"

And he said, "I have been very zealous for the LORD, Lord of Hosts, because the children of Israel have forsaken Your covenant, thrown down Your altars, and killed your prophets with the sword, and I alone am left, and they seek to take my life."

The LORD said to him, "Go, return on the road through the Wilderness of Damascus, and when you arrive, anoint Hazael to be king over Aram. And you shall anoint Jehu, the son of Nimshi, to be king over Israel, and you shall anoint Elisha, the son of Shaphat of Abel Meholah, to be prophet in your place. He who escapes the sword of Hazael will be killed by Jehu, and he who escapes the sword of Jehu will be killed by Elisha. Still, I have preserved seven thousand men in Israel for Myself, all of whose knees have not bowed to Baal and whose mouths have not kissed him."

So he departed from there and found Elisha the son of Shaphat, who was plowing with twelve yoke of oxen before him and he with the twelfth, and Elijah passed by him and threw his cloak on him. He left the oxen and ran after Elijah and said, "Please let me kiss my father and mother, and then I will follow you."

And he said to him, "Go back, for what have I done to you?"

So he returned from following him and took a yoke of oxen and sacrificed them and boiled their flesh with the yokes from the oxen and gave it to the people, and they ate. Then he got up and went after Elijah and ministered to him.

—1 Kings 19:1–21, mev

GOING DEEPER

I love the stories in the Bible—largely because I am so often able to find my own story within them. Here we have a mighty prophet of God who has called down miracles from heaven, like raising people from the dead and shutting up the windows of heaven so it would not rain for three years. Yet even he had a hard time walking with God consistently.

Elijah hit a crossroads of exhaustion and fear. He had just stood strong in the face of the false prophets of Baal and then waited patiently to prove to the people that his God was the one true God. In the end, victory was his reward—but he still crashed emotionally, fatigue and fear coming on him like fierce bandits. Not being able to control his emotions, Elijah ran. He ran from the wicked Queen Jezebel, he ran from his problems, and ultimately he ran from his God.

The Bible is a commentary on itself. In the Book of James we read that "Elijah was a man with a nature like ours" (5:17). He was just like us. He knew what it was to be depressed, disappointed, and discouraged. He had his own struggles and battles that he fought every single day, just like you and me—but God met him in his grief. He ministered to him in his brokenness. God sent an angel to bring food and water to Elijah and told him to rest, for he was getting ready to enter a forty-day fast. This fast would be a time of reevaluation and reflection. This is one of the reasons why we fast—to hit the reset button and prepare ourselves for a shift in seasons.

The Book of James also tells us that Elijah was a man of prayer. James 5:16–18 tells us that Elijah fervently prayed, and it did not rain for three and a half years. Then he prayed again, and rain began to pour down from heaven. If God hears the prayer of an average person like Elijah, given to the same passions and struggles that all of us have, we can take confidence that He will do the same for those of us who pray and believe.

What did God say to Elijah during his forty-day fast? He told him this would be his final chapter as a prophet of God. God led Elijah to a place of conversation and correction, after which He told him who his predecessor would be. This is when God told him Elisha would be the next voice He would use to minister to the people of Israel. Fasting always prepares us for what's next!

Elijah had been a great prophet to the people of God, but now his days were winding down, and God was using the forty-day fast to show him his next assignment. Note that even among the greatest of prophets no one is so intrinsically holy, anointed, or "spiritual" that they outgrow their need for fasting. It is not something we ever graduate from. In fact, the more we grow in the things of God, the more we will need these times of rest and realignment. God was about to disciple Elisha to be the best leader he could be to the children of Israel, but he needed to carve out time for God to prepare him for this next season.

God met Elijah where he was—tired, discouraged, and ready to give up—just as He meets each of us right where we are.

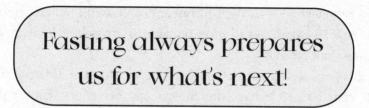

Fasting always prepares us for what's next!

Fasting is not hard labor or an extra chore. Fasting slows us down and opens us up, cleansing our hearts so we can see the things we cannot see on our own. Often, God is already doing the new work all around us, already shifting things, but we don't have the discernment to see what God is doing until we fast. Fasting gives us the gift of recognition and allows us to see the move of God when it comes.

God told Elijah that his assignment was over and he was to anoint Elisha as the next prophet of Israel. It was time for Elijah to get ready for his greatest God encounter yet; he would be taken up by God in a whirlwind to heaven. God was not done with His servant, and He is not done with you either! God has more for you to do, more for you to see, and deeper places He wants to take you.

Fasting will take you deeper than you ever thought possible.

FOR FURTHER STUDY

Consider the pattern given to us in James 5:16–18 of confession of prayer, a pattern of healing and renewal. Reflect on how God might be calling you now to practice what you read in this text.

COACHING THOUGHTS

As we proceed through this week's study, we will compare each daily characteristic to Elijah and his forty-day fast. We will see how God is honest with us even in our times of whining and self-pity, and how He continues to meet our needs—as well as lovingly correct our bad behavior.

This week is a great opportunity for you to take a deeper look into your life. How have the choices and behaviors of your past brought you to where you are today? Course correction is imperative to becoming your best self, and fasting creates an ideal opportunity to change directions.

FASTING FOR
CHARACTER

DAVID

A solid trust is based on a

consistent character.

—JOHN MAXWELL

char·ac·ter | ˈker-ik-tər |

noun

the mental and moral qualities distinctive to an individual

SIGNS OF LACK OF CHARACTER

- You do not value others' time or suggestions.
- You are focused on your agenda.
- You talk about others behind their backs.
- You use people for your own advancement.
- You overpromise but under-deliver.

CHARACTER DEFINES OUR convictions, beliefs, passions, and personality. Trust and influence are built upon a person's character. We are constantly challenged with decisions and emotions that test our character. The key is to be aware of our daily behavior and make good choices. These affect our character and often lead us to new opportunities and possibilities. Character will follow you all the days of your life.

SCRIPTURE PASSAGES

Though David made some terrible and troubling decisions, we also see a spirit of humility and teachability in him that stands in stark contrast to the character of Israel's former king, Saul. As you read today's passage, pay attention to the way that humility shaped David, and think about how God might be shaping humility in you during your fast.

Samuel said to Saul, "You have done foolishly. You have not kept the commandment of the LORD your God, which He commanded you. Truly now, the Lord would have established your kingdom over Israel forever. But now your kingdom will not continue. The Lord has sought for Himself a man after His own heart and the Lord has commanded him to be prince over His people, because you have not kept that which the Lord commanded you."

—1 Samuel 13:13–14, mev

The Lord said to Samuel, "How long will you mourn for Saul, since I have rejected him from ruling over Israel? Fill your horn with oil and go. I will send you to Jesse the Bethlehemite, for I have chosen a king for Myself from among his sons."

Samuel said, "How can I go? If Saul hears it, he will kill me."

And the Lord said, "Take a heifer with you and say, 'I have come to sacrifice to the Lord.' Call Jesse to the sacrifice, and I will show you what you will do. And you will anoint for Me him whom I tell to you."

Samuel did that which the Lord spoke, and came to Bethlehem. The elders of the town trembled at his coming, and said, "Do you come in peace?"

And he said, "I have come in peace to sacrifice to the Lord. Consecrate yourselves, and come with me to the sacrifice." And he consecrated Jesse and his sons and called them to the sacrifice. When they came, he looked on Eliab, and said, "Surely the anointed of the Lord is before Him."

But the Lord said to Samuel, "Do not look on his appearance or on the height of his stature, because I have rejected him. For the Lord sees not as man sees. For man looks on the outward appearance, but the Lord looks on the heart."

Then Jesse called Abinadab, and made him pass before Samuel. And he said, "Neither has the Lord chosen this one." Then Jesse made Shammah to pass by. And he said, "Neither has the Lord chosen this one." So Jesse made seven of his sons pass before Samuel. And Samuel said to Jesse, "The Lord has not chosen these." Samuel said to Jesse, "Are these all your young men?"

And he said, "There remains yet the youngest, and there he is shepherding the flock."

Then Samuel said to Jesse, "Send and bring him, for we will not sit down until he comes here."

So he sent and brought him in. Now he was ruddy with beautiful eyes and a good appearance. And the LORD said, "Arise, anoint him, for this is he." Then Samuel took the horn of oil, and anointed him in the midst of his brothers. And the Spirit of the LORD came on David from that day forward. So Samuel arose and went to Ramah.

Now the Spirit of the LORD departed from Saul and an evil spirit from the LORD terrified him. So the servants of Saul said to him, "See, an evil spirit from God troubles you. Let our lord now tell your servants, who are before you, that they might seek out a man experienced in playing the lyre. And it will come to pass, when the evil spirit from God is on you, that he will play with his hand, and you will be well."

Saul said to his servants, "Find me now a man that can play well, and bring him to me."

Then one from the servants answered, and said, "I have seen a son of Jesse the Bethlehemite, who is experienced in playing music, a mighty man of valor, a man of battle, and skillful in words, even a man of fine appearance. And the LORD is with him."

Therefore Saul sent messengers to Jesse, and said, "Send me David your son, who is with the sheep." Jesse took a donkey laden with bread, a bottle of wine, and a young goat and he sent them with his son David to Saul.

David came to Saul, and stood before him. And Saul loved him greatly and he became his armor bearer. Saul sent to Jesse, saying, "Let David stand before me, for he has found favor in my sight."

It happened that when the evil spirit from God came on Saul, David would take the lyre in his hand and play. So Saul was refreshed and was well, and the evil spirit departed from him.

—1 SAMUEL 16:1–23, MEV

GOING DEEPER

King David was a man after God's own heart. In order to be people of character, we must first submit to the heart of God—to hearing His voice, heeding His plan, and walking in humility. David exhibited these qualities from an early age. As a shepherd boy, he would sit in the pastures looking into the night sky, counting the stars, meditating on God, and singing psalms and praises unto his King. He had a heart that desired to know God.

Having a humble heart, David respected King Saul and was honored when the prophet Samuel asked him to go and play his harp for the king. Saul was often troubled by distressing spirits and needed music to calm his spirit.

I'm not sure David yet fully understood the anointing from the prophet Samuel, but time would soon prove that God had removed His hand from Saul and placed it on David.

It would be years before David would ever sit on the throne, but it was in the pruning years between his anointing and his appointment that God was building character in this man. God was testing him, trying him, proving him, so that He might ultimately promote him.

God saw David's heart and chose him at a young age, but David still needed to be prepared for the challenges that lay ahead. Character is built, not given. You cannot be handed character. You must be strong, steadfast, and determined to build character.

When it was time, David would be king. He was a tremendous leader. As a commander, warrior, confidant, and king, David was known as a mighty man of valor. He had both wisdom and compassion and would be known as the king who brought peace to Israel.

You may know the story of David and Bathsheba and wonder how someone who committed adultery and murder could be a man of valor and character. Yes, David had his flaws and sins, but he was a man who sought after the heart of God. If anything, this story should give us confidence in the fact that our God is gracious and forgiving, quick to redeem and restore.

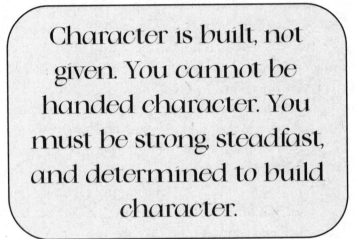

Character is built, not given. You cannot be handed character. You must be strong, steadfast, and determined to build character.

What made David different from so many other leaders who disobeyed and sinned? His heart—his true repentance and humility before God. His brokenness and dependence upon the only One who could truly forgive and restore would ultimately prove to be more defining than his sin.

Read David's confession:

> Have mercy upon me, O God, according to Your lovingkindness; according to the multitude of Your tender mercies, blot out my transgressions. Wash me thoroughly from my iniquity, and cleanse me from my sin. For I acknowledge my transgressions, and my sin is always before me. Against You, You only, have I sinned, and done this evil in Your sight— that You may be found just when You speak, and blameless when You judge....Create in me a clean heart, O God, and

renew a steadfast spirit within me. Do not cast me away from Your presence, and do not take Your Holy Spirit from me.

—PSALM 51:1–4, 10–11

Let me encourage you to examine your heart today. How is your personal character? Who are you when no one else is looking? Are you a man or woman seeking after the heart of God?

David was not afraid to become vulnerable with God. His broken and contrite heart is what proved to be his greatest asset. As God's Spirit reveals truth to you during this time of introspection, I invite you to use David's prayer above as a way to confess your own sin and invite in the newness of God.

FOR FURTHER STUDY

Reflect on the following scriptures, which summon us to a life of character, and ask Holy Spirit to show you how to apply these words to your life right now.

- Proverbs 10:9
- Philippians 4:8
- Proverbs 28:18
- Proverbs 22:1
- Romans 12:2
- Proverbs 11:3
- Romans 8:6
- Colossians 3:23–24

COACHING STEPS

1. The first step to building character is to be honest with yourself. Humility is a quality that accompanies character. Do you find yourself pushing to get ahead of others? Do you monopolize most of the conversations you have, justifying it by saying that you know more than others and that you are just helping to make leaders? The word *humble* comes from the image of a brook that has run dry and is very low. Unless we take the lower seat at the table, we will never be on track to build our character.

2. Trust and loyalty are two key components in a person of character. You do what you say and follow through to the end. If you find yourself making excuses or not being true to your word, you may need to reevaluate your intentions. Think of two or three people you consider loyal and trustworthy. What characteristics do you find attractive and inspiring in them? How do you demonstrate these in your daily life?

3. It is important to continually raise up leaders under our watch. Our choices and behavior are modeled and repeated by those we lead. When you make a mistake or become tempted to choose the wrong path, what you do *next* will make the biggest impact on those watching. Be truthful with your story, and stay close to the heart of God. Good character does not lie; truth will always be revealed.

THE ELIJAH FAST

Elijah was a prophet of God. He, like David, had seen God's mighty hand on many occasions—but he was not immune to grief and sorrow. After he battled the prophets of Baal on Mount Carmel, he felt exhausted and defeated. He moaned and complained that he alone was left to serve God. He had an emotional breakdown. True to God's character, He sent an angel to minister and encourage Elijah. The angel gave Elijah food and water and told him to get some rest before his fast.

Elijah took time to reflect and process as he fasted for forty days.

> So he arose, and ate and drank; and he went in the strength of that food forty days and forty nights as far as Horeb, the mountain of God.
>
> —1 Kings 19:8

Fasting is a time for refuge, a time to refuel. Even while we feel weak in our bodies, it is a time for us, in the words of Jesus in Matthew 11:29, to "find rest for [our] souls."

DISCUSSION QUESTIONS

- Character is a quality that can be tarnished or attributed to discipline and conviction. If you were to rate your integrity and character on a scale of one to ten, how would you do? No one needs to know that answer but you. The true question is, are there areas in your life that you need to bring to God? Take a moment and reflect on the steps of your life. Where might you need to make some course corrections? Write your thoughts below.

- David was anointed king long before he took the throne. Often God uses time as a tool to build our faith and maturity. Is there something you are waiting on from God—an answered prayer, a breakthrough, a healing? Do you believe God will come through? Take a moment now and reflect on the ways God has grown your testimony through the waiting period. Are you waiting on God, or is God waiting on you? Sometimes we are the ones that need to take the next step as a reminder and a way to stay encouraged. Is there anything *you* need to do?

- Elijah was a mighty prophet of God who saw acts of healing and miracles throughout his entire ministry— but he, like all of us, got tired and discouraged. After the heroic display of faith and strength on Mount Carmel, Elijah crashed. It was not his character that was in question; it was his physical and emotional well-being. It is so important to be holistically healthy. How are you doing—body, soul, and spirit? Take some time today and evaluate your well-being. In the space below, give yourself some healthy advice. Where do you need to make some changes?

PRAYER

Dear Lord, my deepest desire is to be a person after Your heart, to walk in humility and integrity, to be a person of contagious character for Your kingdom. Teach me to hear Your prompting and heed Your voice. May my testimony be one that others aspire to follow. In Jesus' name, amen.

JOURNAL ENTRY

FASTING FOR
WISDOM

— SOLOMON —

Wisdom is the right use of knowledge. To know is
not to be wise. Many men know a great deal, and
are all the greater fools for it. There is no fool so
great a fool as a knowing fool. But to know how to
use knowledge is to have wisdom.

—CHARLES SPURGEON

wis·dom | ˈwiz-dəm |

noun

the quality of having experience, knowledge, and good judgment; the quality of being wise

SIGNS OF LACK OF WISDOM

- You care more about the moment than the outcome.
- You don't have the desire to grow or learn anything new.
- You are impulsive and make impromptu decisions.
- You live in past mistakes and memories.
- You are impressed by what the world has to offer.

WE SEE THE depth and expanse of the wisdom of Solomon in 1 Kings 4:29–30: "And God gave Solomon wisdom and exceedingly great understanding, and largeness of heart like the sand on the seashore. Thus, Solomon's wisdom excelled the wisdom of all the men of the East and all the wisdom of Egypt."

Gifts and talents come from God and are to be used and stewarded for His benefit. When we forget where our abilities come from, we risk losing it all.

Aristotle said, "There is a foolish corner in the brain of the wisest man."[1] Solomon received wisdom from God. But time would tell if he could manage it.

SCRIPTURE PASSAGES

Solomon's story demonstrates both the power of walking in divine wisdom and how whether or not we continue in wisdom will always be a choice. As you read today's passage, reflect on your own need for God's wisdom—as well as the times that, like even King Solomon, you have chosen not to walk in it.

> I am going the way of all the earth. Be strong, and show yourself to be a man. And keep the charge of the LORD your God, walking in His ways, keeping His statutes, His commandments, His judgments, and His testimonies, as it is written in the Law of Moses, that you may prosper in all that you do and wherever you turn, that the LORD may carry out His word that He spoke concerning me, saying, "If your children take heed to their way, to walk before Me in faithfulness with all their hearts and with all their souls, you shall not fail to have a man on the throne of Israel."
>
> —1 KINGS 2:2–4, MEV

Solomon loved the LORD, walking in the statutes of his father David, though he sacrificed and burned incense at the high places. The king went to Gibeon to sacrifice there, for that was the great high place, and he offered a thousand burnt offerings on that altar. While he was in Gibeon, the LORD appeared to Solomon in a dream at night, and He said, "Ask what you want from Me."

Solomon answered, "You have shown great mercy to your servant David my father, because he walked before You in faithfulness, righteousness, and uprightness of heart toward You. And You have shown him great kindness in giving him a son to sit on his throne this day. Now, O LORD, my God, You have made Your servant king in place of my father David, and I am still a little child and do not know how to go out or come in. And Your servant is in the midst of Your people whom You have chosen, a great people, so numerous that they cannot be numbered or counted. Give Your servant therefore an understanding heart to judge Your people, that I may discern between good and bad, for who is able to judge among so great a people?"

It pleased the LORD that Solomon had asked this. God said

to him, "Because you have asked this and have not asked for yourself long life or riches or the lives of your enemies, but have asked for yourself wisdom so that you may have discernment in judging, I now do according to your words. I have given you a wise and an understanding heart, so that there has never been anyone like you in the past, and there shall never arise another like you. I have also given you what you have not asked, both riches and honor, so that no kings will compare to you all of your days. If you will walk in My ways, keeping My statutes and My commandments as your father David did, then I will lengthen your days."

—1 KINGS 3:3–14, MEV

GOING DEEPER

Following in the footsteps of a successful and powerful leader is, at best, difficult—especially when the leader is your father. We remember reading the story of David's affair yesterday, and how despite his sin, God continued to use him. Today's story shows the product of that decision. Solomon was the son of David and his maidservant, Bathsheba.

I can only imagine the pressure on this newly appointed king. Solomon knew he had been chosen by both his father, David, and the prophet of God, Nathan—but now he needed wisdom to rule the nation.

The Bible tells us that Solomon married Pharaoh's daughter and brought her back to the City of David so he could complete the building of the house of God. All along, he was sacrificing burnt incense in high places. Then the Lord appeared to Solomon in a dream and said, "Ask! What shall I give you?"

We can see the pull of conviction already playing out in this king's life—he burned incense and asked that God would give him an understanding heart to judge the people. What Solomon was asking for was wisdom.

I love this account precisely because it is so real. The power to make decisions as a king is obvious—but the choice to rely on God for wisdom is brilliant.

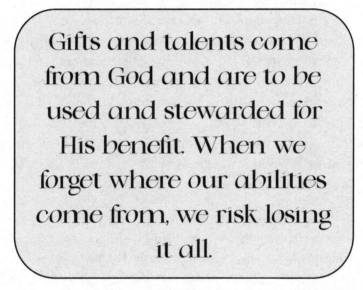

Gifts and talents come from God and are to be used and stewarded for His benefit. When we forget where our abilities come from, we risk losing it all.

Throughout Solomon's reign we see story after story of how wisdom played a part in his kingdom. In 1 Kings 3:16–28, two women came to Solomon for a ruling. Both women lived in the same house, and both had given birth at the same time. One of the children died in the middle of the night, and there was no witness in the house. Both claimed the child that was still alive was theirs.

Solomon, in his wisdom, spoke out for all to hear: "Bring me a sword, and I will cut the baby in two so that each woman can have half a child." (See 1 Kings 3:24–25.) Of course, the true mother yelled out loud, "Oh, King, no! Let her have the baby," thus revealing who the real mother was. The Scriptures say that all Israel heard the judgment and "feared the king, for they saw that the wisdom of God was in him to administer justice" (1 Kings 3:28).

Wisdom is observable. When you walk in the wisdom of God, people see it. In account after account, Solomon led his people in wise choices.

Wisdom cannot be taught or bought—it must be sought. Only God can give us wisdom, and as we will see, it does not come with a lifetime warranty. It must be asked for and received day by day.

As we read about the journey of King Solomon, we see that just as his father, David, he truly did have a heart for God. Still, power and women and success can all add up to making poor choices and a life of ruins.

In 1 Kings 11 we see where wisdom turns to folly, the downfall of Solomon, for he loved many foreign wives and made alliances with other nations:

> But King Solomon loved many foreign women, as well as the daughter of Pharaoh: women of the Moabites, Ammonites, Edomites, Sidonians, and Hittites—from the nations of whom the LORD had said to the children of Israel, "You shall not intermarry with them, nor they with you. Surely they will turn away your hearts after their gods." Solomon clung to these in love. And he had seven hundred wives, princesses, and three hundred concubines; and his wives turned away his heart.
> —1 KINGS 11:1–3

Thus Solomon's legacy in Scripture is complex. He is known for contributing to three different books of the Bible: the Song of Solomon, Proverbs, and Ecclesiastes. It has been said that he wrote Song of Solomon when he was young and enjoyed the pure love of one wife, he wrote Proverbs while he was filled with the wisdom from God, and he wrote Ecclesiastes later in life when he was cynical and discouraged. We can see Solomon's departure from wisdom as he grew older. We can see firsthand that wisdom must be desired daily and can never compete with pride or opulence.

Solomon is still referred to as the wisest king of Israel, but his life choices are what brought him to destruction. We should all heed his writing from Proverbs 19:20: "Listen to advice and accept instruction, that you may gain wisdom in the future" (ESV).

FOR FURTHER STUDY

Spend a few moments reflecting on the following verses that call us to spiritual wisdom. Invite God to show you where and how you need to embrace His wisdom in your own life.

- Proverbs 2:6
- Ephesians 5:15–16
- James 1:5
- James 3:17
- Proverbs 16:16
- Colossians 4:5–6
- Proverbs 13:10

COACHING STEPS

1. The first step toward gaining wisdom is knowing you can't get it on your own. As we said earlier, wisdom cannot be bought or taught—only sought. You must ask God for it. The reason behind your request will determine whether you receive it or not. Only a heart

that seeks after the ways of God will be given true wisdom.

2. On my own prayer walk each day for several years now, I have asked God for three things: insight, wisdom, and revelation. Let me explain: I do not know what lies ahead, but I do know the One who does. So, I ask God to show me in my spirit how to have insight into how to manage my day, wisdom to discern right from wrong, and revelation to know how to prepare for my next steps. When you have a relationship with Christ, you can ask Him to lead, guide, and direct your steps. Do you need to take a walk with God today to talk about some things?

3. Never assume you will always make the right choices. Satan is a roaring lion seeking someone to devour (1 Pet. 5:8). You must use wisdom each and every day to walk with God. One thing I like to say to my coaching clients is that smart people put smarter people around them—that's wisdom. Find someone you can be accountable to, and guard that relationship.

THE ELIJAH FAST

Mentorship is a powerful way to raise up the next generation of leaders. After Elijah had rested and finished his fast, he began to look for his next protégé. Wisdom told him his days were coming to a close. He knew he had to find his replacement. We should always be looking for those we can train and mentor in the faith.

Elijah was a prophet who not only performed many miracles but also had a deep connection with God. Let me ask you: Do others see God lived out in your life? Are you raising up those who will, in turn, raise up others? Take time on your fast today to think of someone you can mentor or meet with to encourage and equip in the things of God. Your fast is your time to go deeper with God and see all He has in store for you.

DISCUSSION QUESTIONS

- The kind of wisdom we see in the reading about Solomon and the two mothers is the kind of wisdom only God can give. Has there ever been a time in your life when God gave you wisdom beyond your own understanding to solve a problem? Share your story below.

- Solomon started his journey as a king spiritually divided. On one side he was entertaining false gods, and on the other side he was asking God for wisdom. James 1:8 tells us that a double-minded person is "unstable in all his ways." We cannot have one foot in the world while the other is in the Word. Have you found yourself struggling between two opinions? You reason to yourself, "Yes, it's OK," when you really know it is not. Take a moment and write down the areas or choices you are currently dealing with that might compromise your walk with God. Only you can ask for wisdom from God.

- In today's fast we talked about how Elijah knew he had to begin looking for his replacement—the one that would carry the mantle of God for the next generation. Let me ask you: Are you doing anything to pour yourself into the next generation? We are living in precarious times, and the Gen Z community is looking for mentors. We need to pray and participate in helping prepare them for their assignment. Who are you training up—a child, neighbor, niece, or nephew? Take a moment and write down a commitment you are making to God about your willingness to do something for the next generation.

PRAYER

Dear Lord, today I learned that I could ask for wisdom—so I ask for it now. I ask for wisdom to make the right choices and to never depart from Your Word. I ask that You give me the strength to say no to temptation and sin, and the foresight to see where the enemy is working. Teach me to know Your Word and walk in Your ways. In Jesus' name, amen.

JOURNAL ENTRY

_____

_____

_____

_____

_____

day
10

FASTING FOR
INTEGRITY

— JOSEPH —

Integrity is the glue that holds our way of life together.
What our young people want to see in their elders is
integrity, honesty, truthfulness, and faith. What they
hate most of all is hypocrisy and phoniness....Let them
see us doing what we would like them to do.

—BILLY GRAHAM

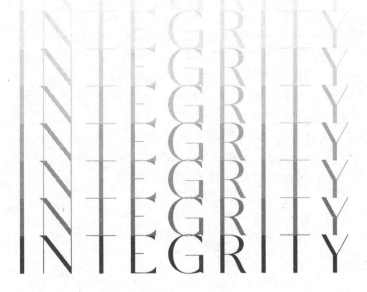

in·teg·ri·ty | in-ˈte-grə-tē |

noun

the quality of being honest and having strong moral principles; moral uprightness

SIGNS OF LACK OF INTEGRITY

- You justify lies and bad behavior.
- You're overly proud and highly arrogant.
- You're defensive and argumentative.
- You're rude and engage in off-color conversation.
- You're unable to ask for forgiveness.

I REMEMBER THE FIRST time I witnessed integrity. I was in the fourth grade and spending the day with my best friend at an amusement park. We had just finished riding the most thrilling roller coaster in the park and were quickly running to the next ride on our list. As we ran past an older gentleman, Jenny noticed that he had dropped a twenty-dollar bill from his pocket. He hadn't noticed, but Jenny did. Now, I might add that a twenty-dollar bill in the '60s was like a hundred-dollar bill today. Immediately Jenny stopped, turned around, and ran back to pick up the money. What would she do next? Keep it, or return it to its rightful owner? I'm sure you know the answer to my question—that's why it made such an impact on a young fourth-grade girl. Doing what is right is always the right thing to do. Yes, she returned the money to the elderly man, and we went on our way, skipping with laughter to the next ride for the day.

SCRIPTURE PASSAGE

Joseph had the opportunity to indulge his flesh when no one else was looking, but he chose to do the right thing. Whether or not we walk in this kind of integrity will determine the kind of people we will become. As you read today's passage, ask God how He wants to speak into your own integrity during this fast.

Now Joseph was brought down to Egypt, and Potiphar, an officer of Pharaoh, captain of the guard, an Egyptian, bought him from the Ishmaelites who had brought him down there.

The LORD was with Joseph, so that he became a prosperous man. He was in the house of his master, the Egyptian. His master saw that the LORD was with him and that the LORD made all that he did to prosper. Joseph found favor in his sight and served him. So he made him overseer over his house, and all that he had he put under his charge. From the time that he had made him overseer in his house and over all that he had, the LORD blessed the Egyptian's house on account of Joseph. So the blessing of the LORD was on all that he had in the house and in the field. So he left all that he had in Joseph's charge, and he had no concerns regarding anything except the food he ate.

Now Joseph was handsome and well-built. After a time, his master's wife took notice of Joseph and said, "Lie with me."

But he refused and said to his master's wife, "My master does not concern himself with anything concerning me in the house, and he has committed all that he has to my charge. There is none greater in this house than I. He has kept nothing back from me but you, because you are his wife. How then can I do this great wickedness and sin against God?" She spoke to Joseph every day, but he did not listen to her about lying with her or being with her.

But it happened one day that Joseph went into the house to do his work, and none of the men of the house was there. She caught him by his clothing, saying, "Lie with me." But he left his clothing in her hand and fled and got outside.

When she saw that he had left his clothing in her hand and had fled outside, she called to the men of her house and spoke to them, saying, "See, he has brought in a Hebrew among us to humiliate us. He came in to me to lie with me, and I cried out with a loud voice. When he heard that I lifted up my voice and cried out, he left his clothing with me, fled, and got outside."

She laid up his clothing next to her until his master came home. She spoke to him using these words, saying, "The Hebrew servant, whom you have brought to us, came in to me to mock me. When I lifted up my voice and cried out, he left his clothing with me and fled outside."

When his master heard the words of his wife, which she spoke to him, saying, "This is what your servant did to me," he became enraged. Joseph's master took him and put him into the prison, a place where the king's prisoners were confined.

So he was there in the prison. But the LORD was with Joseph and showed him mercy and gave him favor in the sight of the keeper of the prison. The keeper of the prison committed all the prisoners that were in the prison to the charge of Joseph. So whatever they did there, he was the one responsible for it. The keeper of the prison did not concern himself with anything that was under Joseph's charge because the LORD was with him. And whatever he did, the LORD made it to prosper.

—GENESIS 39:1–23, MEV

GOING DEEPER

Integrity will take you from a shepherd boy to the second in command under the king. Integrity is doing what you know is right. This was a valuable lesson Joseph would learn along the journey of life. From being thrown in a pit, to being sold into slavery, and then being thrown into jail for something he did not do—God was cultivating integrity in this man.

Joseph was set up by Potiphar's wife. She made advances toward him that he did not embrace. This was a man of true integrity. But pride got the best of this woman, and she had him falsely accused of impure behavior. The next thing we see, Joseph is behind prison bars for something he did not do—but this is where God would prove him and test him and use him, and finally exalt him.

Once again, the hand of God was on Joseph in prison. The guard said, "Anything Joseph has his hand on, I do not need to worry about." (See verse 23.) Joseph had the trust of others—even the prison guard—because he had integrity.

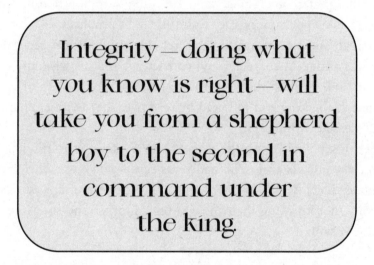

Integrity—doing what you know is right—will take you from a shepherd boy to the second in command under the king.

One common thread we see in the stories of Joseph is that he was a man who told the truth. To be a person with integrity, you must tell the truth.

Earlier, in Genesis 37, God gave Joseph a dream in which the stars, the sun, and the moon bowed down to him. God was speaking to Joseph through his dreams. He was giving him a prophetic vision to hold on to through the difficult years, teaching him that the day would come when he would be used as a leader in Israel—a day when his eleven brothers, and even his father, would all come and bow down to him. This would not come about because he was royalty but because God placed him in a position to provide for all of Israel.

On another occasion, while Joseph was in prison, he met the butler and the baker of the king. They, too, had been imprisoned. Both the baker and the butler had dreams while in prison, and God allowed Joseph to interpret them: the butler would go back into the kingdom to serve Pharaoh, but the baker would die. Joseph told the truth whether the message was kind or not.

Years later, when Pharaoh had dreams that no one could interpret, the butler remembered Joseph. He told Pharaoh about Joseph, "the interpreter of dreams," and the king summoned him from prison. This put him in place to fulfill God's prophecy.

Joseph was not afraid to interpret the king's dream accurately. He was a man of character and conviction, and his wisdom came from God. He told the king there would be seven years of abundance in the kingdom followed by seven years of famine. Pharaoh was pleased with Joseph.

At this point we see the stage being set for the fulfillment of the prophetic vision Joseph had years earlier, for it was during the famine that Joseph's brothers and father came and bowed down to him, not knowing that this was their brother and son. Genesis 41:39–41 says:

> Then Pharaoh said to Joseph, "Inasmuch as God has shown you all this, there is no one as discerning and wise as you. You shall be over my house, and all my people shall be ruled according to your word; only in regard to the throne will I be greater than you." And Pharaoh said to Joseph, "See, I have set you over all the land of Egypt."

FOR FURTHER STUDY

Your fast is a time during which God will sharpen your integrity. Reflect on these scriptures that invite us to live with integrity, and invite Holy Spirit to throw His light on your own shadows as you read them.

- Proverbs 11:3
- Proverbs 20:7
- Galatians 6:7
- 1 Peter 3:16
- Proverbs 12:22
- Luke 6:31
- Psalm 41:11–12

COACHING STEPS

1. The first step to developing personal integrity is taking responsibility for your own actions. Honesty comes naturally to those who walk with integrity. Begin to take notice of your actions when you're confronted with a challenge. Do you take responsibility, or do you find someone else to be your scapegoat?

2. Equally important as being responsible is showing respect to others. Over the last three years the pandemic has paved a pathway for disrespect and dishonor. We have all seen it play out on our streets and even in our homes. Take a moment today and

reevaluate your thoughts and responses toward others. Do you need to make a change in your conversations or actions? A person of integrity is comfortable with course correction.

3. Are you reliable? By that I mean are you a person of your word, someone who follows up and follows through with your commitments? One of the greatest compliments someone can give you is, "They are a person of their word." It is better to not overcommit than it is to overcommit and not follow through. Take some time now and look at your calendar and personal schedule. Are there things you should delegate to someone else? Never feel you must do everything. The most important lesson here is to only do those things you can truly commit to.

THE ELIJAH FAST

Elijah had to do some soul-searching during his forty-day fast. In this part of his story he was worried, tired, and maybe even mad at God. Again, God will meet us where we are. It is important that you be honest with God during your fast. I am sure you have already discovered some areas in your life that you would like to grow and develop—maybe even the area of integrity.

Did you notice in 1 Kings 19:4–8, one of our Scripture passages from Day 8, that an angel brought Elijah food and water and told him to sleep and get some rest? Elijah was exhausted and could not make rational decisions. God wants us to be healthy and whole. Integrity starts with being honest with where you are *today*. Are you running from God? Do you possibly need to get some rest?

DISCUSSION QUESTIONS

- Would you say you are a person of integrity? Only you would truly know what is in your heart. Only a person of true integrity can walk away from temptation. Take a moment right now and think of a time you said no to the enemy. It is important to remind ourselves of the good decisions we have made in our lives rather than simply rehearsing the bad ones. It empowers us to make the right choices now to walk in right standing with God.

- Joseph was not afraid to be honest with Pharaoh when interpreting his dream. Often we feel pressured into telling people what they want to hear rather than telling them the truth. Do you struggle with peer pressure? You may need to ask God to strengthen your ability to be honest with others. Take some time today and review your last few conversations. Were you honest with your responses? If not, how could you have responded with both truthfulness and kindness? Write your response below.

- Today we talked about the sheer exhaustion Elijah felt after running from Jezebel. We read that the angel of the Lord came to Elijah, brought him water and bread, and told him to rest. Self-integrity knows when it's time to take a break. Are you tired or discouraged or maybe even doubting God? Be good to yourself today. Take time to truly rest in the presence of God and embrace your fast. This is a special twenty-one-day journey to get to know who God destined you to be. Take a moment and share what you are asking God for over these days together.

PRAYER

Dear Lord, thank You for creating me in Your image. You knew me in my mother's womb. You saw me in my unframed state, yet You gave Your life to redeem me. I ask that You use me for Your kingdom and Your cause. I pray I will walk in integrity all the days of my life. Lord, lead and guide me so I do not go astray. In Jesus' name, amen.

JOURNAL ENTRY

_____

_____

_____

_____

_____

_____

_____

FASTING FOR
VISION
DEBORAH

Give to us clear vision that we may know where to
stand and what to stand for, because unless we
stand for something, we shall fall for anything.

—PETER MARSHALL

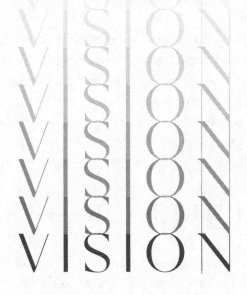

vi·sion | ˈvi-zhən |

noun

the ability to think about or plan the future with imagination
or wisdom

SIGNS OF LACK OF VISION

- You are afraid to take uncomfortable risks.
- You cannot accept change.
- You do not embrace new ways to tackle a problem.
- You are limited by fear.
- You are comfortable with the status quo.

HELEN KELLER IS often quoted as saying, "The only thing worse than being blind is having sight but no vision."[1] Both deaf and blind, she defied all odds by going to school and earning her bachelor's degree, learning to communicate in a way that impacted the lives of millions of people around the world. Why? Because she had vision beyond sight.

In the Book of Proverbs we read a powerful declaration: "Where there is no vision, the people perish" (29:18, KJV). *Perish* is a strong and bold word, but I believe it is exactly the right word for the concept. It means to die. People without vision, without insight from God, will indeed perish—they will dry up and blow away. In the days in which we currently live, we need vision to make the right choices and see what is happening right before our very eyes.

SCRIPTURE PASSAGES

The two women in today's passage from Judges chapter 4 show us the power of vision to change everything. As you see the clarity and perspective they operate with here, ask God to give you the gift of vision for the battles you are facing in your own life.

When Ehud was dead, the children of Israel once more did what was evil in the sight of the LORD. The LORD sold them into the hands of King Jabin of Canaan, who ruled in Hazor. The commander of his army was Sisera. He lived in Harosheth Haggoyim. The children of Israel cried out to the LORD, for Sisera had nine hundred iron chariots and had forcefully oppressed the children of Israel for twenty years.

Now Deborah, the wife of Lappidoth, was a prophetess. She judged Israel at that time. She would sit under the palm tree of Deborah between Ramah and Bethel in the hill country of Ephraim. The children of Israel would go up to her for her to render judgment. She sent for Barak son of Abinoam from Kedesh in Naphtali and said to him, "The LORD God of Israel commands you, 'Go and deploy troops at Mount Tabor, and take ten thousand men from the tribes of Naphtali and Zebulun with you. I will draw Sisera, the commander of the army of Jabin, with his chariots and large army to you at the River Kishon and give him into your hands.'"

Barak said to her, "If you will go with me, then I will go, but if you will not go with me, then I will not go."

She said, "I will indeed go with you. However, the way you are going will gain you no glory, for the LORD will deliver Sisera into the hand of a woman." Then Deborah got up and went with Barak to Kedesh. Barak called Zebulun and Naphtali to Kedesh. Ten thousand men went up on foot with him, and Deborah went up with him also.

Now Heber the Kenite had moved away from the Kenites, who were descendants of Hobab, Moses' father-in-law. He pitched his tent at the oak in Zaanannim, near Kedesh.

Then they told Sisera that Barak son of Abinoam had gone up to Mount Tabor. So Sisera summoned all his nine hundred iron chariots and all the people with him, from Harosheth Haggoyim to the River Kishon.

Then Deborah said to Barak, "Get up, for this is the day that the LORD has given Sisera into your hands. Has not the LORD gone out before you?" So Barak went down from Mount Tabor with ten thousand men behind him. The LORD routed Sisera and all of his chariots and all of his army with the edge of the sword in front of Barak. Sisera dismounted his chariot and fled on foot.

Barak chased after the chariots and the army as far as Harosheth Haggoyim. The whole army of Sisera fell by the edge of the sword. Not a single man survived. Sisera fled on foot to the tent of Jael, the wife of Heber the Kenite, for there was peace between King Jabin of Hazor and the family of Heber the Kenite.

Jael went out to meet Sisera and said to him, "Turn aside, my lord. Turn aside to me. Do not be afraid." So he turned aside to her into the tent, and she covered him with a rug.

He said to her, "Please give me a little water to drink, for I am thirsty." So she opened a leather milk container, gave it to him to drink, and covered him.

He said to her, "Stand in the entrance to the tent, and if anyone comes and asks you, 'Is there a man here?' then you say, 'No.'"

Then Jael the wife of Heber took a tent peg and a hammer in her hand and went quietly to him, for he was fast asleep and tired. She drove the tent peg into his temple, and it went down into the ground, so he died.

Now as Barak had been chasing Sisera, Jael came out to meet him and said, "Come, and I will show you the man whom you seek." When he came in, there was Sisera fallen dead with a tent peg in his temple.

So God humbled King Jabin of Canaan before the children of Israel that day. The children of Israel grew more and more powerful over King Jabin of Canaan until he was no more.

—JUDGES 4:1–24, MEV

> In those days there was no king in Israel; everyone did what
> was right in his own eyes.
>
> —JUDGES 21:25

GOING DEEPER

Wow! These are two women of such insight and wisdom. Deborah was a prophetess appointed by God. She was the only female judge mentioned in the Bible, and she had authority in both civil and religious affairs. People would come to her with disputes as well as for wisdom.

Deborah had grown tired of King Jabin's oppression of the children of Israel, and she had the insight to see that it was time for action—something had to change. Deborah called for the commander of Israel to come to meet with her, ordering him to take ten thousand men, along with the armies she would deploy, to take out the enemy.

Deborah had a vision from God of how this battle would end. She was willing to hear Barak out, and she assured him she would go along with him. She then followed up with a proclamation that the Israelites would indeed win the war—in fact, it would be won by the hands of a woman. But she was not the woman she was referring to.

What is it about vision that makes people want to follow and attach themselves? Vision is truly a contagious concept. This story is full of intrigue and suspense, but it also shows the foresight Deborah had to take control of the situation. When you come to a point when you say enough is enough, you will begin to gain vision for the next steps to take. The first step is always the hardest, but also the most important. Deborah could see the children of Israel free and out of captivity. She took action and came up with a plan.

Only God could have arranged the circumstances for a woman

named Jael to become the hero of the story. Barak did not have the vision of Deborah; he was calculated and insecure and not the one to lead the charge. There is nothing wrong with taking others along with you for the battle, but when you are the person for the job, you must have enough vision to lead the way. We see from the story that the armies were at war, pursuing one another in battle, but God was also working. God is always working alongside us in our battles.

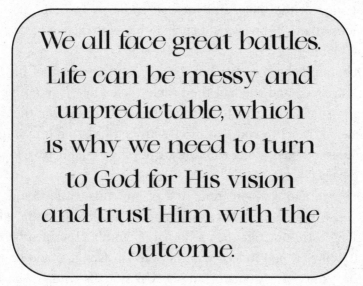

We all face great battles. Life can be messy and unpredictable, which is why we need to turn to God for His vision and trust Him with the outcome.

Sisera, the enemy commander, was worn out and needed some rest. Arriving at what he thought was neutral territory, he approached the house of a young woman, requesting a place to rest and for her to guard the door while he slept. This warrior was no match for a woman with vision. Although she was not involved with either of the opponents, she knew that Sisera was not a good man. Vision will give you wisdom beyond your natural under-standing. Ideas, strategies, and even favor come from God when we seek His ways.

Jael knew Sisera was tired, and she knew he felt safe in her home. She also knew he was a threat to Israel. After inviting him to lie down and drink some warm milk, she covered him with a blanket and assured him she would watch the door. Then, once he was sound asleep, she took a tent peg and a hammer and quietly drove the peg into his temple.

As Barak made his way toward Jael's house, she motioned for him to come and see where the body of Sisera lay. Immediately Barak understood Deborah's prophecy that the Lord would sell Sisera into the hands of a woman. The history of Israel was secure for the next forty years, all because Deborah had the vision to fight the battle with the wisdom of God.

We all face great battles. Life can be messy and unpredictable, which is why we need to turn to God for His vision and trust Him with the outcome. Did you know that God had a plan for your life before you were even born? Proverbs 19:21 says, "There are many plans in a man's heart, nevertheless the LORD's counsel—that will stand."

It is imperative that we seek the plans of God for our lives. You might be saying to yourself right now, "I don't have vision to see beyond today. I don't know how to see what God is doing." Can I tell you that's OK? You are right where God wants you: knowing you need Him to help you—that you need Him for insight, wisdom, and revelation. That's why we are on this journey together—to make a change, to grow more into the likeness of Christ and become the people God created us to be. Are you ready to see what God sees? Are you ready to grow in spiritual vision? If your answer is yes, then get ready; God is getting ready to open your eyes.

FOR FURTHER STUDY

As these scriptures illuminate the role of vision in our lives with God, ask God to illuminate your own life with His vision. The fast is an ideal opportunity to be opened up, to see things you have not yet seen and hear things you have not yet heard!

- 2 Kings 6:17
- Habakkuk 2:2
- Proverbs 29:18
- Habakkuk 2:3
- Joel 2:28
- Daniel 7:13–14
- Jeremiah 29:11
- Amos 3:7

COACHING STEPS

1. Have you ever been around someone who just had a big vision? Their plans were detailed, their convictions were strong, and they could rally the troops at the drop of a hat. That's a person with vision. They know the outcome is worth the effort. Oh, to be a person with vision! But how do we get there? First, you must let go of the fear of failure. Fear cripples vision every time. Take a moment and reflect upon the times you quit a task because of fear. The only way to overcome fear is with faith—faith that God

is with you in the moment and that He will see you through to the end.

2. A second deterrent to vision is being unwilling to change. Think about our story today: Deborah had to be willing to do something different in order to see a new outcome. Change is hard, even scary at times, but it is the only way to move from point A to point B. You must pick up your feet and actually move in a new direction. You must have a different viewpoint to see a new outcome. What action steps can you take today to begin to see change occur in your life?

3. Status quo is the sign of a person who will never grow or go to new levels of self-development. Life is predictable and comfortable, just the way they like it. "Don't disrupt my foundation," they say, "I don't want to have to rebuild my life." That mindset is limiting and will keep you from ever seeing the vision God has for your life. Have you become comfortable with your routine as it is, or do you long for more? That is the question you must ask yourself before you can move deeper with God.

THE ELIJAH FAST

Elijah was a man of vision before he lost his way with fear. He had seen God move in a powerful way on Mount Carmel, but Jezebel's threats had him in hiding and isolation. Fear and isolation are tools the enemy uses to rob you of your faith. Take some time today to sit alone with Jesus. "If any of you lacks wisdom," James 1:5 says, then "ask of God, who gives to all men liberally" (MEV).

I like to tell people that fasting is feasting at the feet of Jesus.

Today is a good day to recommit your fast unto God. You are fasting for a change. I am sure you have identified many things in your life that you may like to change thus far. For today, though, let's just sit in the silence of the moment and ask God for His vision for our future. Be still and let God speak. He is never in a hurry. He likes it when we come just as we are.

DISCUSSION QUESTIONS

- Vision keeps us motivated and passionate. Are you a dreamer? Would you say you are a person who has vision? It takes confidence and strategy to pull off an idea. What is something that you have personally executed and seen to completion? Share your memory below.

- Deborah was the only woman in the Bible who was called to be a judge. I would think she could have been a little proud or entitled by that position, yet she led with humility and honor. She allowed Barak to stay the commander and Jael to be the woman known in the Bible for winning the war for Israel. Vision is never competitive. A true leader with vision encourages others. Are you tempted to take the limelight when you are right? Take a moment and think about how you handle your success. Do you brag, or do you bow? Write your response below.

- In our fasting story today we talked about what fear can do to cripple vision. Elijah fell under threats from Jezebel and hid in the desert. He lost his confidence and boldness, and he no longer shared the same vision God had for him. It is vitally important that we stay committed to the plans and calling God has for our lives. Have you lost your God-given vision? If so, recommit yourself to God today. His plans, His purpose, and His vision for your life truly are the best. What do you think God wants you to do for the kingdom?

PRAYER

Dear Lord, today I come to You asking for vision. I want to see what You see for my life. I want to have faith and not fear for where You desire to take me. I ask that You teach me to be humble and to honor those around me. Fill me with the Holy Spirit. I want to grow deeper in my walk with You. In Jesus' name, amen.

JOURNAL ENTRY

_____

_____

_____

_____

_____

_____

day
12

FASTING FOR
PATIENCE
JOB

Some of your greatest blessings come with patience.

—WARREN WIERSBE

Teach us, O Lord, the disciplines of patience, for to
wait is often harder than to work.

—PETER MARSHALL

pa·tience | ˈpā-shən(t)s |

noun

the capacity to accept or tolerate delay, trouble, or suffering without getting angry or upset

SIGNS OF LACK OF PATIENCE

- You're unable to sit still for an extended period.
- You interrupt others so you can talk.
- You act before the appropriate time.
- You often make impromptu decisions.
- You expect others to see your viewpoint and agree with you.

PATIENCE IS NOT a quality that comes naturally for most people—but it is one that can be developed. The first step in learning patience is being patient.

It has been said that good things come to those that wait—and now they can prove it. Scientific research has found that patience can extend your life by lowering your blood pressure, relaxing your heart rate, and stabilizing your daily stress. Patient people were less likely to report things like headaches and ulcers. The same research went on to report that people with type A personalities were more likely to have health issues and were more sleep deprived.[1]

A common idiom about patience is "Patience is a virtue." The phrase is thought to originate from the poem "Piers Plowman," written by William Langland around the year 1360. It meant to be able to wait for something without becoming frustrated.

Well, a little insight into this author: that's not me. I must confess this is an area in which I need change. I was born in high gear. I am always on the move and looking for where I need to go next. And yes, I am type A. Let's look together at the ways we need to change to become people who value and embrace patience.

SCRIPTURE PASSAGES

The story of Job is the biblical primer on patience. When we fast, we have to sit with our problems, vulnerabilities, and frailties rather than just repressing them or pretending everything is OK. These times of reflection can be full of pain as well as joy. But it is precisely as we learn to sit with pain, grief, and questions that God cultivates patience within us. As you read the story of Job, reflect on how God might want to use this time to grow this virtue in you.

And the LORD said to the Adversary, "Have you considered My servant Job, that there is none like him on the earth, a blameless and an upright man, who fears God, and avoids evil?"

Then the Adversary answered the LORD, saying, "Has Job feared God for nothing? Have You not made a hedge around him, around his household, and around all that he has on every side? You have blessed the work of his hands, and his possessions have increased in the land. But stretch out Your hand now, and touch all that he has, and he will curse You to Your face."

The LORD said to the Adversary, "Look, all that he has is in your power; only do not stretch out your hand against his person."

So the Adversary departed from the presence of the LORD.

So a day came when his sons and his daughters were eating and drinking wine in their eldest brother's house, and a messenger came to Job and said, "The oxen were plowing, and the donkeys were feeding beside them, and the Sabeans attacked them, and took them away, and they killed the servants with the edge of the sword, and only I alone have escaped to tell you."

While he was still speaking, another came and said, "The fire of God fell from heaven and burned up the sheep and the servants and consumed them, and I alone have escaped to tell you."

While he was still speaking, another came and said, "The Chaldeans formed three companies and made a raid on the camels and have taken them away. They killed the servants with the edge of the sword, and I alone have escaped to tell you."

While he was still speaking, another came and said, "Your sons and your daughters were eating and drinking wine in their eldest brother's house, and suddenly a great wind came from the wilderness and struck the four corners of the house, and it fell on the young people, and they are dead; and I alone have escaped to tell you."

Then Job stood up, tore his robe, and shaved his head. He fell to the ground and worshipped. He said, "Naked I came from my mother's womb, and naked will I return there. The LORD gave, and the LORD has taken away; blessed be the name of the LORD."

In all this Job did not sin, and he did not accuse God of wrongdoing.

—JOB 1:8–22, MEV

The Adversary answered the LORD, saying, "Skin for skin; yes, all that a man has he will give for his life. Put forth Your hand now and touch his bone and his flesh, and he will curse You to Your face."

The LORD said to the Adversary, "Very well, he is in your hand, but spare his life."

Therefore, the Adversary went out from the presence of the LORD, and he afflicted Job with severe sores from the sole of his foot to the top of his head. So he took a piece of broken pottery with which to scrape himself while he was sitting among the ashes.

His wife said to him, "Are you still maintaining your integrity? Curse God and die."

He said to her, "You talk like one of the foolish women talks. Will we indeed accept the good from God but not accept the adversity?"

In all this Job did not sin with his lips.

—Job 2:4–10, MEV

GOING DEEPER

Someone who demonstrates great restraint is often referred to as "having the patience of Job." They tend to manage trials, setbacks, pain, and annoyances with noble perseverance.

You may feel like you have had a hard day, but let's go toe to toe with the story of Job and see who has more patience.

First off, Job lost all his children and his wealth in a single day. Then, his body became covered with painful boils, and his wife turned her back on him, telling him to curse God and die. Next, Job's three friends came to console him, but they did not even recognize him. They reasoned in their hearts that Job had turned his back on God, and so they quickly turned their backs on Job.

Still, in all of this, Job did not sin. Job 2:10 records his response to his wife: "But he said to her, 'You speak as one of the foolish women speaks. Shall we indeed accept good from God, and shall we not accept adversity?' In all this Job did not sin with his lips."

Job was getting ready to go on a journey with God—not one he asked for, nor one he would have chosen for himself, but one that would prove to be the greatest revelation of God's love and mercy.

Often when we go through times of difficulty or pain, we ask God what we did wrong. We examine our lives and try to be better people. In truth, however, sometimes our afflictions are meant to bring us closer to God, to bring us closer to knowing who we are.

There are also times that our struggles leave us feeling alone and isolated. People will judge us and determine that we have sinned or behaved in an ungodly manner to receive such punishment—but the reality is that God is in the heartbreak, bringing us deeper into the knowledge of His will.

> The purpose of the Book of Job is to show us that God will go to great lengths to teach us about how loved and protected we are, even when the opposite seems to be the case.

The purpose of the Book of Job is to show us that God will go to great lengths to teach us about how loved and protected we are, even when the opposite seems to be the case.

Job endured heartbreak, loss, pain, rejection, and doubt. But his faith in an all-consuming God prevailed. In the last chapter of Job, his final hour reveals how patient Job truly was.

Consider Job's response to God:

> Then Job answered the LORD and said: "I know that You can do everything, and that no thought can be withheld from You. 'Who is he who hides counsel without knowledge?' Therefore I have uttered what I did not understand, things too wonderful for me which I did not know. Hear, and I will speak; I will

question you, and you declare to Me.' I have heard of You by the hearing of the ear, but now my eye sees You. Therefore I abhor myself, and repent in dust and ashes."

—JOB 42:1–6, MEV

And now read the blessing God gave Job in response to his obedience and patience:

So the LORD blessed the latter days of Job more than his beginning, for he had fourteen thousand sheep, and six thousand camels, and a thousand yoke of oxen, and a thousand female donkeys. He had also seven sons and three daughters. He called the name of the first Jemimah; and the name of the second Keziah; and the name of the third Keren-Happuch. In all the land, there were no women as beautiful as the daughters of Job, and their father gave them an inheritance along with their brothers. After this, Job lived a hundred and forty years, and saw his sons, and their sons to the fourth generation. So Job died, being old and full of days.

—JOB 42:12–17, MEV

In light of God's extraordinary vindication of Job and the extravagant blessings He gave him, yes, I would indeed say patience is a virtue. This is one area in which I am personally trying to improve. How about you?

FOR FURTHER STUDY

Meditate on the following scriptures that invite us to live patient lives. Even as you read them, allow yourself to slow down—don't rush to the next thing, but instead fully embrace this moment and the God who wants to meet you in it.

- Proverbs 14:29

- Romans 12:12

- Galatians 6:9

- Psalm 37:7

- Exodus 14:14

- Psalm 27:14

COACHING STEPS

1. Slow down. You must make yourself take a step back—that may mean walking slower, talking slower, or doing less. If you are prone to doing things quickly, this will be difficult. But I promise you it will pay off in the long run.

2. Practice subtraction before addition. This is one of my coaching assignments for my clients: take something off your plate before you can add something to your plate. We must learn to reduce our yeses. Often we struggle with patience because we are too busy. Doing less is best, especially if you find yourself frustrated and hyperactive.

3. Allow others to have a voice. People who are impatient often finish others' sentences, overtalk, and get antsy with slow conversations. They dominate dialogue and justify it by deciding that what they have to say is either better articulated or more important. Learn to see the person speaking as valuable and worthy of your time. Be a good listener.

THE ELIJAH FAST

Elijah had to go through the process of waiting. Even after his forty-day fast he was still angry with God. We find Elijah in a cave when the word of the Lord came to him and asked, "What are you doing here, Elijah?"

Elijah responded with self-pity and pride: "I have been very zealous for you, Lord, and for the children of Israel, but they have forsaken you and turned away. I alone am left, and they come to seek me." (See 1 Kings 19:10.)

Rather than simply rebuking Elijah, God, in His patience, reminded Elijah that he was not alone, that there were still seven thousand who had not bowed down to Baal. Fear and frustration will cause us to run and hide in a cave of self-pity and regret. Today we will turn our eyes toward patience and ask God to show us His plan for our lives.

Take a moment to meditate upon Psalm 27:14: "Wait on the LORD; be of good courage, and he shall strengthen your heart; wait, I say, on the LORD" (KJV).

DISCUSSION QUESTIONS

- In our story today we read about a man who was tempted and tried yet remained true to his God. Do you find yourself questioning God—and maybe even getting angry at Him—when you go through adversity? Take a moment to look back over your journey. When was a time that God walked you through the fires of life and brought you through safely and securely?

- Job's close friends turned their backs on him in his time of greatest need. This often happens because people don't know how to handle their heartache and pain. Our friends may distance themselves out of uncertainty about how to respond. Have you lost a friend because of a hard time you went through? Take a moment and pray for them today. The only way to be completely set free and healed of past hurt is to give it over to God. Prayer can heal a broken relationship, as well as a bruised heart. Remember, your fast is a time for healing.

- Fasting is a spiritual discipline that refines the motives of our hearts. Your fast is an offering to God. It is a tool God will use to help draw you into a deeper relationship with Him. Have you seen God on a deeper level through your fast? Share your insights below. Remember, this is a process, not a race. Take time to slow down and meditate on God. He will show up and speak to you.

PRAYER

Dear Lord, today I ask You for patience. I know I have been anxious and busy with my own plans and desires. I ask that You teach me how to slow down and hear from Your heart. Teach me the discipline of waiting on You to silence my soul and simply rest in Your word. In Jesus' name, amen.

JOURNAL ENTRY

day 13

FASTING FOR GROWTH

PAUL, BARNABAS, and JOHN MARK

Change is inevitable,

growth is intentional.

—GLENDA CLOUD

growth | grōth |

noun

the process of increasing in physical size

the process of developing or maturing physically, mentally, or spiritually

SIGNS OF LACK OF GROWTH

- You have not changed your appearance or mindset in decades.
- You resist new ideas and concepts.
- You are headstrong and set in your ways.
- You fear failure, so you freeze.
- You don't know how to change.
- You believe that where you are is what's best for you now.

CONFRONTATION WILL ALWAYS play a role in our relationships. Being human is hard, and with it comes *personality*. We are taught in Scripture not to rely on our flesh but to be led by the Spirit of God. This comes through maturity and a heart that longs to know God.

In our story today we find three men who all love God. They each had personal encounters with Jesus, yet they find themselves at odds with one another. The strong-willed Paul meets the tender, kindhearted Barnabas, and they can't seem to agree about the young and immature John Mark. Their strong opinions cause them to part ways. It will be years before they reconnect, but only after they independently grow and lay down their personal agendas.

SCRIPTURE PASSAGES

No amount of devotion to God and no amount of practice in the spiritual disciplines makes us exempt from complex, messy human relationships and the sheer friction that comes from simply having different personalities. Today's passage is a very human, accessible look at the relational conflict within the early church. As you read, reflect on the challenging relationships in your own life and think about how God might use this fast to adjust your perspective on them.

> Now the multitude of those who believed were of one heart and one soul; neither did anyone say that any of the things he possessed was his own, but they had all things in common. And with great power the apostles gave witness to the resurrection of the Lord Jesus. And great grace was upon them all. Nor was there anyone among them who lacked; for all who were possessors of lands or houses sold them and brought the proceeds of the things that were sold, and laid them at the apostles' feet; and they distributed to each as anyone had need. And Joses, who was also named Barnabas by the apostles (which is translated Son of Encouragement), a Levite of the country of Cyprus, having land, sold it, and brought the money and laid it at the apostles' feet.
>
> —ACTS 4:32–37

> Saul, still breathing out threats and murder against the disciples of the Lord, went to the high priest, and requested letters from him to the synagogues of Damascus, so that if he found any there of the Way, either men or women, he might bring them bound to Jerusalem. As he went he drew near Damascus, and suddenly a light from heaven shone around him. He fell to the ground and heard a voice saying to him, "Saul, Saul, why do you persecute Me?"
>
> He said, "Who are You, Lord?"
>
> The Lord said, "I am Jesus, whom you are persecuting. It is

hard for you to kick against the goads." Trembling and astonished, he said, "Lord, what will You have me do?" The Lord
said to him, "Rise up and go into the city, and you will be told
what you must do."

—Acts 9:1–6, mev

After some days Paul said to Barnabas, "Let us return and visit
our brothers in every city where we preached the word of the
Lord and see how they are doing." Barnabas determined to
take with them John, who was called Mark. But Paul thought
it was not good to take with them one who had withdrawn
from them in Pamphylia and had not gone with them to the
work. Then there arose a sharp contention, so that they separated from each other. Barnabas took Mark and sailed to
Cyprus, but Paul chose Silas and departed, being commended
by the brothers to the grace of God. And he went through
Syria and Cilicia, strengthening the churches.

—Acts 15:36–41, mev

Only Luke is with me. Get Mark and bring him with you, for
he is useful to me for ministry.

—2 Timothy 4:11

GOING DEEPER

Today's story takes us on a slightly different path because it is a
story of three followers of Jesus who didn't always see eye to eye.
The focus of our fast is not only vertical but also horizontal—God
will use this time to adjust the way we approach all of our relationships. We will learn to navigate the process of building relationships while at the same time growing and developing as individuals.

In any conflict situation, we must always take into consideration
three defining elements:

1. The age and maturity of the individual

2. The temperament and personality of the individual

3. The individual's level of spiritual growth

Let me set the stage for how these three elements operate.

After the crucifixion of Jesus, many joined the movement with the apostles to share the message of Christ. Barnabas was a wealthy man who'd sold all he had and brought the money to the apostles to further the spread of the gospel. He was kind, gentle, and known as the son of consolation and encouragement (Acts 4:36). He became known as an apostle of Christ and shared the message of Jesus' resurrection with all who would hear.

Paul was the former Saul of Tarsus who persecuted Christians. He was called a zealot and a murderer. So, obviously we can see he was a passionate man. He was on the road to Damascus en route to kill all those who followed "the Way" (Jesus) at the time of his conversion—God had a different plan for his life. Struck with blindness, he had an encounter with the God of all sight and quickly converted to "the Way" he once so desperately despised. His conversion and confession led him to become "the apostle Paul," a man as passionate about saving the Christians as he'd once been about trying to murder them. Paul arrived on the scene with the other apostles. They were filled with the Holy Spirit and on fire for God. They had but one mission—to convert everyone to Christ.

John Mark (Acts 12:12), known as Mark in the Gospels, was much younger than the other disciples, possibly only in his teens. His mother was a devoted follower of Jesus who would often open her home for prayer or meetings. Mark grew up watching the story of Jesus unfold. He was educated and believed to be both the translator and the writer for the disciple Peter. Later in life, he traveled with Peter to Rome and stayed with him while he was in prison. Oh, did I mention he was the cousin of Barnabas?

As you can see, we have three completely different individuals called and committed to the cause of Christ: all good men, all commissioned by God, yet all at various levels and stations in life.

Today we pick up the story where Paul and Barnabas were disputing whether or not to take Mark with them on the journey. Barnabas, being the man of encouragement that he was, wanted to take Mark under his wing and help him grow up in the things of Christ.

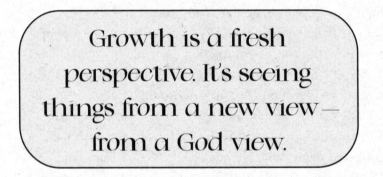

Growth is a fresh perspective. It's seeing things from a new view— from a God view.

Paul, on the other hand, saw Mark as a liability and a weighty burden to the group. "Cut ties with him," Paul responded to Barnabas. "We have too much work to do to take Mark along."

Barnabas disagreed: "What would Jesus do?" He tried to reason with Paul. Mark was young and immature, and maybe he even brought some drama. "But aren't we here to help raise up the next generation? To be salt and light to all those who need our help? Besides, he is my cousin, and I feel responsible for him." (See Colossians 4:10.)

The two could not see eye to eye, and because of this, they parted ways. Paul joined the team with Silas, and Barnabas took Mark, and off they went in opposite directions. This was a season where Barnabas mentored Mark in the stages of maturity. It was time for Mark to stop making excuses and trust that even in difficult times, God would be there to help him. He may have been overly protected by his mother, but if he wanted to be one of the followers of Jesus, Barnabas knew he would need to grow in strength.

In hindsight, we can see how God used both teams for His glory. The gospel was spreading, and the kingdom was advancing. And all three men were growing in their walk with God. Mark was maturing, Paul was bending, and Barnabas was getting stronger. As with most relationships, personal growth can mend the hardest of hearts.

I love 2 Timothy 4:11. Paul was growing older and imprisoned, but he was still leading behind bars and putting pieces in place for the next stage of the journey. He told his young student, Timothy, to be sure to find Mark and bring him along. "Get Mark and bring him with you, for he is very useful to me for ministry." God can restore even the most damaged relationship and make all things new.

Growth is paramount in spiritual maturity. All three of these followers of Jesus needed to see their situation with a fresh set of eyes. Growth is a fresh perspective. It's seeing things from a new view—from a God view. Whatever stage of life you are currently in, you can still grow. There is so much more God has in store for you.

FOR FURTHER STUDY

The following scriptures help us see the need for growth. As you read them, ask God to show you areas where you need to grow, and open yourself up to the ways He is using this fast to stretch and challenge you.

- Proverbs 1:5
- Luke 2:4
- 2 Peter 3:18
- 1 Peter 1:2–3
- Psalm 92:12
- 1 Corinthians 13:11

- Philippians 1:6

- Proverbs 22:6

COACHING STEPS

1. The first step in personal development and growth is desire. Most of us are comfortable with where we are, often even justifying our behavior. You will never go to the next level if you cannot see beyond yourself. Identify areas of weakness that are keeping you stuck, such as pride, knowledge, or laziness. Now, what steps can you take to admit you need to grow and become the person God created you to be?

2. Next, you must lay down your preconceived ideas about others. Your way of doing something is not the only way, and at times it may not even be the best way. I have learned over the years that if I am open to new ideas and concepts, it will benefit me, and I can become a better version of myself. Growth comes by learning and stretching.

3. Become a good listener. Stop and listen to others. Ideas, convictions, and strategies all come when we are open to listening. When you are set in your ways, you stifle the opportunity to learn. Take a moment and think about areas in your life in which you have grown and developed. How did your growth begin? I assume it began with an idea you heard about or a desire you had. All these things begin with listening and being open to others. This is where your journey begins. How can you be a better listener?

THE ELIJAH FAST

Although Elijah had a setback, he did not stay there. His circumstances were preparing him to shift from the role of mentor to mentee. Elijah was getting ready to train up Elisha in the ways of God. Sometimes we don't even know what our fast is doing for us, but then, in a moment's time, a breakthrough comes pushing open the door of opportunity. Elijah had grown through his search for God, and now he could lead the way for the next generation of prophets. Growth is something we don't always notice until we turn around and look back at where we have come from. On your fast today, take some time to reevaluate your progress.

DISCUSSION QUESTIONS

- We don't often stop to think about the characters in the Bible being human and fallible, but they were. Like you and I, they had weaknesses, insecurities— even favorites. The truth is that we all need to grow and mature on our life's journey. Did you see something in our story today that showed you an area of growth in your life? Share your thoughts below.

- Today we looked at three different personality types: Paul, strong and overly controlling; Barnabas, encouraging but possibly enabling; and Mark, young and immature. Out of these three descriptions, whom did you most relate with? You may have elements of all three. In the space below, write down the area of growth you need to develop.

- I love this story because it illuminates the human side of even the ones we think of as "saints." The gospel of Jesus, the good news, needs to be told—but we all have different ways of spreading it. Some are bold, some are soft, and some are new in their learning, but we all are called to share. Who have you shared the gospel with? With whom have you shared the joy of your salvation? If you have never had the privilege of sharing Christ with someone, then make that commitment today. If you truly desire to share Christ, God will open the door for you to walk through. In the space below, write down the name of the individual or individuals with whom you are willing to share Christ. Now, start by praying for them. Begin to tell them about your spiritual journey. God will do the rest.

PRAYER

Dear Lord, I must confess I have not been diligent in self-development. I have been gliding along, too busy to see areas of personal growth. I ask that You show me where I need to grow to be the person You created me to be. I know You have given me gifts and talents that I have not pursued. Lord, help me to stop making excuses and discipline myself for growth in Your Word and in Your plan for my life. In Jesus' name, amen.

JOURNAL ENTRY

_____

_____

_____

_____

_____

_____

_____

_____

_____

_____

_____

_____

_____

_____

_____

day
14

FASTING FOR
RESPONSIBILITY

LYDIA

The greatest day in your life and mine is when we take total responsibility for our attitudes. That's the day we truly grow up.

—JOHN C. MAXWELL

Today's church wants to be raptured from responsibility.

—LEONARD RAVENHILL

re·spon·si·bil·i·ty | ri-ˌspän(t)-sə-ˈbi-lə-tē |

noun

the opportunity or ability to act independently and make
decisions without authorization

SIGNS OF LACK OF RESPONSIBILITY

- You do not follow through with tasks.
- You do not seize opportunities quickly.
- You blame others for your lack of growth.
- You are comfortable living with disorder.
- You justify being too busy to help others with their
  needs.

SOME PEOPLE ARE just born with it—there are those who, even
from childhood, are responsible for themselves: homework,
chores, sports, and so on. But those people are rare; most of us have
to work at following up with our commitments. We must choose
discipline over laziness or lack of interest. This is one of those character traits that falls 100 percent in our lap. Being both self-aware
and observant of the environment we find ourselves in is how we
build responsibility.

Today we find a story of a woman who looked out for the well-
being and needs of those around her. She took an interest in others
and knew how to respond in love. Let's meet Lydia.

SCRIPTURE PASSAGE

Lydia was a woman who modeled the virtue of responsibility, so
often lacking in our time. As you read her story, reflect on the
ways that embracing responsibility enabled her to impact the lives

of others. Be open to how God may be calling you to step into a greater sense of taking responsibility for your own life during your fast.

> From Troas we set sail on a straight course to Samothrace and the next day to Neapolis, and from there to Philippi, which is the main city of that part of Macedonia, and a colony. We stayed in this city several days.
>
> On the Sabbath we went out of the city to a riverside, where prayer was customarily offered. And we sat down and spoke to the women who had assembled. A woman named Lydia, a seller of purple fabric of the city of Thyatira, who worshipped God, heard us. The Lord opened her heart to acknowledge what Paul said. When she and her household were baptized, she entreated us, saying, "If you have judged me to be faithful to the Lord, come to my house and remain there." And she persuaded us....
>
> When it was day, the magistrates sent the sergeants, saying, "Release those men." The prison guard reported these words to Paul, saying, "The magistrates have sent to release you. Now therefore depart, and go in peace."
>
> But Paul said to them, "They have publicly beaten us, who are uncondemned Romans, and have thrown us into prison. And now do they secretly throw us out? Certainly not! Let them come themselves and bring us out."
>
> The sergeants reported these words to the magistrates, and they were afraid when they heard that they were Romans. So they came and entreated them. And they brought them out, asking them to leave the city. They went out of the prison and entered the house of Lydia. When they had seen the brothers, they exhorted them and departed.
>
> —Acts 16:11–15, 35–40, MEV

GOING DEEPER

We don't read much about Lydia in the Bible, but her story impacted several key people. This just goes to show how our lives can make such a difference in humanity and in history if we take responsibility for our opportunities.

As was the case for so many, Lydia was searching for the truth. She had heard the message of Jesus—that He was the way, the truth, and the life—and she wanted to know more. Her first step of responsibility was to herself. She hungered to find salvation, and God heard her cry. At the same time she was searching, God was moving.

The apostle Paul had been attempting to preach in Asia Minor when Holy Spirit spoke to him in a dream and redirected him to Macedonia to bring the gospel to Europe. Paul and Silas made their way to a nearby riverbed in Philippi where they heard people gathered for prayer. Hungry and not yet satisfied, Lydia held on to every word Paul spoke. Yes, she said when she heard the message of salvation, I do believe; I do receive this Messiah. Lydia is assumed to be the first convert for Christ in Europe.

But Lydia's story does not stop there. She was a woman of great wealth and great influence. Her response after salvation was to care for those who were of Christ. She invited Paul and Silas and their team to be guests in her home. From what we read about this woman, it seems that was very typical of the way she lived her life. Scripture is clear to say that when she and her household were baptized, she invited them to stay in her home, indicating she was a person who genuinely cared for others. She ensured all of her household was with her, truly leading them to the message of Christ.

Not only was it Lydia's responsibility to seek out God and lead others on the same pathway, but she was also a woman of wealth, known in her community as a business leader. Macedonia, now part of modern Greece, was known for its textiles, specifically the color purple. God had gifted Lydia the ability to make money and acquire a large home for herself and those she saw who were in need.

I believe God blesses responsibility. I have seen over the years that those who are generous with their resources grow in ways that are not explainable. The increase that God gives His children who are responsible with their gifts and abilities is a guarantee from His Word.

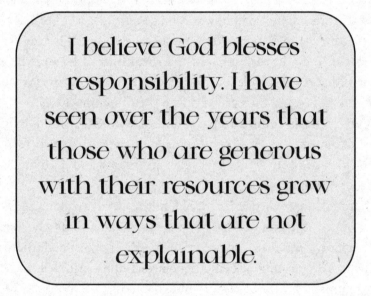

I believe God blesses responsibility. I have seen over the years that those who are generous with their resources grow in ways that are not explainable.

Remember the definition we started with for *responsibility*? "The opportunity or ability to act independently and make decisions without authorization." It is incumbent upon us to take responsibility for our choices, decisions, and opportunities as well as for meeting the needs, hopes, and desires of those we come in contact with.

We pick up the story of Lydia in verse 35, after Paul and Silas have been falsely accused, thrown in prison, beaten, and condemned. I love that Paul knew his governmental rights as a Roman citizen and refused to go away quietly. He asked for those in charge to come and admit that what they had done was wrong and not lawful—another example of being responsible, knowing your governing rights and laws, and not being afraid to speak up.

After they were released from prison, Paul and Silas went back to Lydia's home to be refreshed and to regroup for their next assignment.

The kind of responsibility we see throughout this story is a virtue we often lack. As a pastor and life coach, I have heard my fair share of sad stories about people who don't seem to get a break or are faced with complication after complication. Although these cases do occur, they do so less often than we think. I believe the real issue is that many people look for excuses to blame others for where they are in life and thus stay stuck in their circumstances.

Our modern culture is truly one of entitlement and indifference. According to Forbes, a Gallup poll states that 70 percent of employees are actively disengaged—no interest, no accountability, no responsibility.[1]

I am not sure when it happened, but somewhere along the road we stopped teaching our kids how to work, how to do chores and pick up for themselves, and to see the needs of others and find ways to help. The benefits of being responsible don't just bless us, they bless humanity. Allow the story of Lydia to inspire you today to see the needs of those you cross paths with. Only God knows the outcome of your obedience.

FOR FURTHER STUDY

All of the following verses reveal the weight of responsibility we must bear in order to grow and change. Prayerfully read them, allowing these words to spur you on to embrace the kind of healthy responsibility that will change not only you but also the world around you.

- Romans 14:12
- Proverbs 22:6
- Galatians 6:5
- 1 Corinthians 13:11
- James 4:7
- Luke 16:10
- Colossians 3:23
- Proverbs 6:6
- Romans 14:1
- James 4:17

COACHING STEPS

1. The first step toward becoming more responsible is to become self-aware. Unless you look for ways to change, you never will. Being intentional about new strategies and behaviors is key to self-development. We each must have a desire to become a better version of ourselves. Ask yourself this question: Am I willing to put in the time and make the effort to grow and change? Confirm that in your mind first, or you will never follow through with your commitment.

2. Keep a daily journal of your actions. Not until you begin to see your behavior will you do anything

about it. Record your answers to these three questions each day for six weeks:

    1. How did I take responsibility to personally live healthy today?

    2. Whom was I responsible for helping today?

    3. What actions did I take to encourage someone today?

3. Legacy is the best test of responsibility. Those who follow in our footsteps, whether they be family, friends, or colleagues, will build upon the foundation we have built for them. We must be intentional about our testimony and convictions. If you think back on those individuals who spoke into your life, I think you will agree some were helpful, and others...not so much. You have a responsibility to be life-giving and inspiring to the next generation.

THE ELIJAH FAST

Can you imagine the responsibility of being a prophet of God? I understand that it requires a calling and a spiritual gift from God— but think about how weighty and lonely it must have felt at times. Elijah had to stay close to God to discern His prophetic promptings. He knew he was speaking on God's behalf. To be a prophet took commitment and the confidence that you were truly hearing from God.

In our coaching time today we talked about leaving a legacy for those following in our footsteps. Elijah had to be responsible for his choices. Sometimes we take our spiritual responsibility to grow and mature in the ways of Christ too lightly. Accountability, discipleship, church attendance, and prayer are all ways we take responsibility for our spiritual development.

DISCUSSION QUESTIONS

- Today we read the story of an influential woman who had a hunger for God. It doesn't matter what your financial status is in life—we all need a relationship with Christ. Lydia was responsible for not only her own spiritual journey but those of the members of her household as well. Have you had an encounter with Christ? Recall the power of that moment. Now think of someone you can share your faith with. List the name or names of those you will talk to about Christ. Responsibility starts with you saying yes.

- Not only did Lydia share Christ with others, but she also shared all she had: her home, her resources, and her reputation. Paul and Silas were prisoners, and yet she still brought them into her home. In today's culture it is easy to look the other way and not notice the needs around us, but a person with a gracious heart feels a sense of responsibility for others. Take a moment now and think about how you are helping those in need—possibly working with the homeless or a local charity, or volunteering with a sports club or maybe even at your church. We all can give time to touch the lives of others. Make a list of ways you have served others in the past. Now, what can you do today to reach out and be the hands and feet of Christ?

- Leaving a legacy is something we all aspire to do. As we have read, Elijah walked side by side with Elisha to teach him the ways of God. Whom are you presently coaching or mentoring? Again, part of responsibility is taking the time to invest in others. This might also be a good time to stop and thank those who have poured into your life. Make a list below of those you personally want to thank as well as those in whom you are currently investing. This list will reveal a lot about the journey you are on.

PRAYER

Dear Lord, today I came face to face with my personal responsibility not only for myself but also to others. Father, I ask that You teach me to see the needs of those around me. I want to be a good example to others in my testimony as well as my legacy. I choose to make a commitment to be faithful and disciplined with my choices. Thank You for all the gifts and benefits You have blessed me with. In Jesus' name, amen.

JOURNAL ENTRY

_____

_____

_____

_____

week three

FASTING WITH JESUS

A S WE FAST in order to change, facing down our own demons, history, and temptations, there is no greater model for us than Jesus Himself, who also stared down the forces of darkness during a consecrated time of fasting. As you read this, consider the battles and temptations that are surfacing during your own fast and how the example (and power) of Jesus can equip you to face them without fear.

SCRIPTURE PASSAGE

Jesus, being filled with the Holy Spirit, returned from the Jordan and was led by the Spirit into the wilderness, being tempted by the devil for forty days. During those days He ate nothing. And when they were ended, He was hungry.

The devil said to Him, "If You are the Son of God, command this stone to become bread."

Jesus answered him, "It is written, 'Man shall not live by bread alone, but by every word of God.'"

The devil, taking Him up onto a high mountain, showed Him all the kingdoms of the world in a moment of time. And the devil said to Him, "I will give You all this power and their glory, for it has been delivered to me. And I give it to whomever I will. If You, then, will worship me, all will be Yours."

And Jesus answered him, "Get behind Me, Satan! For it is written, 'You shall worship the Lord your God, and Him only shall you serve.'"

He brought Him to Jerusalem, set Him on the pinnacle of the temple, and said to Him, "If You are the Son of God, throw Yourself down from here. For it is written: 'He shall give His angels charge concerning you, to preserve you.'"

—LUKE 4:1–10, MEV

GOING DEEPER

Jesus' forty-day fast in the wilderness is one of the most powerful stories in the Bible, for it is where we learn firsthand how to stand against the wiles of the devil. Jesus had just been baptized by John the Baptist when He saw the heavens opening and the Spirit of God descending like a dove upon Him. Then He heard a voice from heaven saying, "This is My beloved Son, in whom I am well pleased" (Matt. 3:17). God was confirming His Son. I might add that this passage is a beautiful picture of the Trinity: God the Father, Son, and Spirit.

Immediately after Jesus was baptized, the Spirit sent Him into the wilderness. It is there, while Jesus was fasting and preparing for His earthly ministry, that we see the three temptations Satan brought to Him. Did you know that it was the Spirit of the Lord that led Jesus into the wilderness to be tempted by the devil? As it often goes in Scripture, powerful experiences of God are followed by times of testing, training, and preparation. It was not Satan but the Holy Spirit that drove Jesus into the wild—as it is the Spirit who has drawn you into the wild now.

The same Spirit that just a few verses before descended upon Jesus with confirmation and blessing also took Him into the lonely place. God is showing us that Jesus was fully God and fully human at the same time. It was the human Jesus that was tempted and tested and resisted the devil. Three times Satan came to Jesus with fleshly temptations, and three times Jesus quoted Scripture back to him.

Satan will always tempt you in one of three ways, and it is during times of fasting that we gain the clarity to recognize these temptations for what they are:

- The lust of the flesh—to turn the stones into bread; to satisfy the hunger Jesus felt in His body

- The lust of the eyes—to become a spectacle; to show off; to make an outward display of power in order to "prove Himself"

- The pride of life—the temptation to yield to ego and vanity

We get the language to name these three categories from 1 John 2:16: "For all that is in the world—the lust of the flesh, the lust of the eyes, and the pride of life—is not of the Father but is of the world." Sin is never original; the packaging of the temptations changes, but their essence stays the same, fitting the same template that we see in the wilderness.

Satan waits for the perfect moment to come and tempt you. Did you notice his timing in coming to talk to Jesus right at the beginning of His fast? But Jesus turned it around and used it to grow His strength. Fasting will increase your strength and give you the wisdom to know how to battle the enemy.

It was no mistake that the Spirit of God led Jesus into the wilderness—the place where we are not weaker but actually stronger—during His forty-day fast. This was the very place where Jesus would win the battle with the enemy. Jesus taught us that to do warfare with Satan, we must know the Word of God. We are not wise enough to battle the enemy on our own; we must know how to use Scripture as our weapon.

It is also important for us to notice what happens in this final section of Scripture: the devil flees, and angels come and minister to Jesus. When we stand strong and use the Word of God, Satan will always flee. Then, as we stand strong, we experience comfort from sources we could not have imagined before the wilderness. Did you know you have ministering angels? God is always with you, and His angels are here to protect you. We may face a heightened sense of conflict with the enemy when we are battling in the wilderness during our fast, but we will also find comfort we could not have known before.

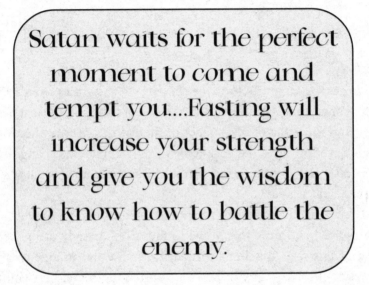

Satan waits for the perfect moment to come and tempt you....Fasting will increase your strength and give you the wisdom to know how to battle the enemy.

Remember, Jesus started His public ministry right after His forty-day fast. This shows me that if I am facing something big or difficult, or if I am in need of some type of change in my life, I should consider beginning the process with a fast. If Jesus began His mission with a fast, I think it might be a good idea for us to follow His lead!

I pray this is not just a one-time commitment on your part, but rather that fasting becomes a regular part of your spiritual exercise, discipline, and the rhythm in your life with God.

FOR FURTHER STUDY

Whatever battles, struggles, and conflicts are being highlighted for you on this wilderness journey, you are not alone. Jesus has already faced it all, and He is facing all of this alongside you and in you now. As you read the following passages, take comfort from the image of the One who sees us, knows us, and gives us the power to overcome as He overcame.

- Hebrews 4:15

- 1 Peter 5:8–9

- Ephesians 6:10–12

COACHING THOUGHTS

In our last week together, we are going to look at seven different characteristics that, if applied to our lives, will make us more like Christ—peace, discipline, wonder, compassion, self-control, generosity, and humility.

As we contemplate these healthy characteristics, we will use Jesus' own forty-day fast as our point of reference. We will see how Jesus battled the enemy in the wilderness by applying wisdom and strategy.

Our fast is to be a weapon and part of our spiritual armor to win against the attacks of the enemy. Remember to take your time and process each coaching concept and discussion question.

God has something new to teach you this week. Your breakthrough is coming!

day
15

FASTING FOR
PEACE

MARY, THE MOTHER
OF JESUS

A great many people are trying to make peace, but that
has already been done. God has not left it for us to do;
all we have to do is to enter into it.

—DWIGHT L. MOODY

Man is not at peace with his fellow man because he is
not at peace with himself; he is not at peace with
himself because he is not at peace with God.

—THOMAS MERTON

peace | ˈpēs |

noun

freedom from disturbance; tranquility

SIGNS OF LACK OF PEACE

- You are anxious and fidgety.
- It is hard for you to silence the noise in your head.
- You cannot let go of unforgiveness.
- It is difficult for you to rest with God.
- You are always looking for what will go wrong with your day.

IF I WERE hard-pressed, I would have to admit that today's reading is one of my favorite Bible stories. There is just something about this simple maiden girl being chosen to give birth to the Son of God that makes the salvation story so precious. I don't believe we can find a better person to represent the quality of peace than Mary, the mother of Jesus. Just think about how she responded after the heavenly symphony declared the birth of the Messiah. Angels and heavenly hosts were singing, shepherds were watching, prophecy was being spoken—and this young new mother sat quietly pondering all these things in her heart (Luke 2:19). That, to me, is true peace: the ability to enjoy this moment of awe and wonder even after giving birth in a stable. Mary would learn to rely on this peace for many years to come, for her Son was indeed the Prince of Peace.

SCRIPTURE PASSAGES

While we often relegate these wonderful stories of Mary to the Christmas season, they give us a powerful model of how to walk in peace no matter where—or when—we are. As you read today's passages, be attentive to the peace in Mary, and think about how God might be calling you to follow her example during your fast.

In the sixth month the angel Gabriel was sent from God to a city of Galilee named Nazareth, to a virgin betrothed to a man whose name was Joseph, of the house of David. And the virgin's name was Mary. The angel came to her and said, "Greetings, you who are highly favored. The Lord is with you. Blessed are you among women."

When she saw him, she was troubled by his words, and considered in her mind what kind of greeting this might be. But the angel said to her, "Do not be afraid, Mary, for you have found favor with God. Listen, you will conceive in your womb and bear a Son and shall call His name JESUS. He will be great, and will be called the Son of the Highest. And the Lord God will give Him the throne of His father David, and He will reign over the house of Jacob forever. And of His kingdom there will be no end."

Then Mary said to the angel, "How can this be, since I do not know a man?"

The angel answered her, "The Holy Spirit will come upon you, and the power of the Highest will overshadow you. Therefore the Holy One who will be born will be called the Son of God.

—LUKE 1:26–35, MEV

And in the same area there were shepherds living in the fields, keeping watch over their flock by night. And then an angel of the Lord appeared to them, and the glory of the Lord shone around them, and they were very afraid. But the angel said to them, "Listen! Do not fear. For I bring you good news of great joy, which will be to all people. For unto you is born this day in the City of David a Savior, who is Christ the Lord. And this will be a sign to you: You will find the Baby wrapped in strips of cloth, lying in a manger."

Suddenly there was with the angel a company of the heavenly host praising God and saying, "Glory to God in the highest, and on earth peace, and good will toward men."

When the angels went away from them into heaven, the shepherds said to each other, "Let us now go to Bethlehem and see what has happened, which the Lord has made known to us."

So they came hurrying and found Mary and Joseph, and the Baby lying in a manger. When they had seen Him, they made widely known the word which was told them concerning this Child. And all those who heard it marveled at what the shepherds told them. But Mary kept all these things and pondered them in her heart. The shepherds returned, glorifying and praising God for all the things they had heard and seen, as it had been told them.

—LUKE 2:8–20, MEV

GOING DEEPER

I would like for you to loose this story from the confines of the Christmas season. There are so many truths we fail to see because we think we already know the passage, but I promise you there is so much more to glean from the story you think you know.

This was a time in history when there was much fear and uncertainty. It was around 4 BC, and the Jews (including Mary and Joseph) were living under the dictatorship of Caesar Augustus and his vast Roman empire, and under the violent reign of King Herod, who ruled over Jerusalem and Bethlehem. This was the same Herod who had his wife killed, his wife's father killed, his wife's brother killed, his own three sons killed, and three hundred of his own military leaders killed.

Herod was evil and he hated the Jews; he was determined to threaten them and make them feel inferior to his power. Yet the

Jewish people managed to keep to themselves and maintained their faith and reverence for God. They certainly held to the promise found in Leviticus 26:6: "I will give peace in the land, and you shall lie down, and none will make you afraid; I will rid the land of evil beasts."

Much like today, the rulers of this time loved to control and count their subjects; people were seen as numbers and minions to be watched and ruled. Caesar Augustus ordered a census that everyone must register in their hometown by a certain time. This meant that Mary, who was nine months pregnant, would have to accompany Joseph to Bethlehem to be counted—a brutal journey approximately eighty miles from Nazareth in Galilee to northern Bethlehem. To make matters worse, Mary would make the journey riding on a donkey.

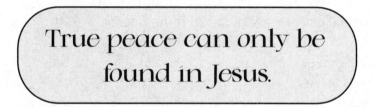

True peace can only be found in Jesus.

Bethlehem was typically a quiet little community, but with all the Jews returning home for the census, lodging would be a problem—unless you had the Prince of Peace traveling with you. After finding no room at any local inn, Joseph could hear Mary quietly whisper, "I think it's time." A stable would become the birthplace of the Messiah, the King of the Jews. It should not surprise us that Jesus was born with the lowly, for the Scriptures tell us in advance, in Isaiah 7:14, "Therefore the Lord Himself will give you a sign: Behold, the virgin shall conceive and bear a Son, and shall call His name Immanuel [God with us]."

Even in all this, Mary and Joseph were not forgotten by God, for He had sent a heavenly host of angels to them to witness the birth of the Christ-child and bring the glowing announcement to the world. Scripture tells us that Mary kept all these things and pondered them in her heart. That is the true definition of peace: not being reactive but trusting God in the midst of uncertainty and difficulty. Mary took refuge in the words of promise and comfort the angel had spoken over her life: "Do not be afraid, Mary, for you have found favor with God."

Finding complete peace in the middle of crisis and conflict is not easy—actually, it is impossible without the peace of God. You try breathing exercises, relaxation classes, meditation, and maybe even denial, but you are left with a stress-filled heart and a longing for true peace, because true peace can only be found in Jesus.

Listen to what Jesus said to His disciples in John 16:33: "I have told you all this so that you may have peace in me. Here on earth you will have many trials and sorrows. But take heart, because I have overcome the world" (NLT). In his book *Mere Christianity*, C. S. Lewis writes, "God cannot give us a happiness and peace apart from Himself, because it is not there. There is no such thing."[1]

The biggest takeaway from this story is the presence of peace in the midst of chaos. Mary was believed to be a young girl, possibly even a teenager, yet she found resolve in knowing God was working on her behalf. We are fasting for a change in our lives. Do you need to find peace? It begins with knowing God is with you and that no matter what trials or uncertainty comes your way, you can find rest for your soul. (See Matthew 11:28–29.)

Mary and Joseph undoubtedly encountered judgment and ridicule from others—and we know they felt isolated and separated from friends and family. Yet through it all they had the peace of God. Have you ever experienced that kind of peace? You can, by walking in the Spirit of the living God. His name is Jesus.

FOR FURTHER STUDY

The following verses all lead us into God's peace. As you read them, allow the Spirit of God to breathe God's peace into you. Drink in the comfort of His presence as you drink in these words.

- Leviticus 26:6
- Numbers 6:24–26
- Psalm 4:8
- Psalm 29:11
- Psalm 34:12–14
- Psalm 37:10–11
- Psalm 119:165
- Proverbs 12:20
- Isaiah 26:3–4
- Matthew 5:9
- John 14:27

COACHING STEPS

1. Peace is a concept that most of us find attractive. When we observe someone who is calm and collected, we assume they must have a stress-free life—but that is not always the case. Some people have just learned how to manage their emotions and situations. They can tell when life is getting too busy or a conflict is rising. They have discovered the art of de-stressing

and resting, two elements that are keys to living at peace. First, you must de-stress. That means you stop and evaluate each problem, circumstance, or complication before it gets out of control, choosing how to handle it before it handles you. Second, you stop and pray. You ask God to give you wisdom and insight on how to move forward, and you ask Him to fill you with His Spirit of peace.

2. You must remove yourself from negative, toxic people. You cannot live a life of rest and joy if you have surrounded yourself with people who drain you. Like-minded people tend to do life together. That means you must stop and take an inventory of whom you are associating with. If you want to have peace and harmony in your home, find healthy people to speak into your life.

3. Stop blaming yourself or your circumstances for your unhappiness. I like to say in my coaching practice, "You are where you want to be. If not, you would find a way out." We do what our deepest desire calls us to do. Everyone can experience peace. We must do the work to become our best selves and allow Holy Spirit to fill our hearts with His love.

THE JESUS FAST

Today we start week three of our fast, transitioning to the forty-day fast of Jesus. As we read earlier, Jesus was led into the wilderness by the Spirit to be tempted by the devil. Even in the midst of enemy attacks, Jesus stayed calm and restrained.

Satan was strategic in trying to take Jesus' attention away from

His fast. With one test after another the enemy relentlessly plagued Jesus with questions and temptations—and he is no different with us. Satan always aims to distract us. We must remain focused and faithful during our fast together. Take a moment now and rest in the assurance that you are surrounded by the peace of God. We have all authority and power to speak against the enemy and proclaim our victory in Christ.

DISCUSSION QUESTIONS

- Today's story is known as the Christmas story, and while it is obviously the story of Christ's birth, it is so much more: it is a story about finding peace along the journey of life. The God of all peace calls us by name and created us in His image. Take a moment right now and thank Jesus for giving you life abundantly. You can rest in confidence that the Maker of the heavens and the earth walks with you day by day, step by step. Thank Him for His love.

- Have you ever just sat quietly with God—no words or music or motion? Just you and God? It is difficult to sit in silence and solitude, but this spiritual discipline is life changing. At first you may struggle to get through even five minutes. But with time and experience you will learn to turn your eyes upon Jesus and see things that can't be seen in the natural realm. That is true peace—seeing what God has to show you. Try to sit for two to three minutes right now and just allow the Holy Spirit to meet you. Be patient and rest in the silence.

- The quote from Thomas Merton that we started today with rings so true: "Man is not at peace with his fellow man because he is not at peace with himself; he is not at peace with himself, because he is not at peace with God." We must learn to be at peace with ourselves, our lives, our choices, our family, and our friends. Turmoil and anxiety only lead to stress and heartache. Take a moment now and check your happy monitor. Do you have joy and peace in your heart? If not, ask God to show you where you need to ask forgiveness or make a course correction. Make things right with the world—and then with God. This is your moment to take an internal look. What do you see?

PRAYER

Dear Lord, I long to have the kind of peace that only You can give. Please teach me to trust Your leading and walk in step with You. Teach me how to better handle my adversity and to practice good self-care and spiritual discipline in my life. I want to walk in Your peace. In Jesus' name, amen.

JOURNAL ENTRY

_____

_____

_____

day
16

FASTING FOR
DISCIPLINE

PAUL

It was character that got us out of bed, commitment that moved us into action, and discipline that enabled us to follow through.

—ZIG ZIGLAR

The battle of prayer is against two things in the earthlies: wandering thoughts and lack of intimacy with God's character as revealed in His word. Neither can be cured at once, but they can be cured by discipline.

—OSWALD CHAMBERS

dis·ci·pline | ˈdi-sə-plən |

noun

orderly or prescribed conduct or pattern of behavior

self-control[1]

SIGNS OF LACK OF DISCIPLINE

- Your responsibilities go unfinished.
- Your office, home, car, etc., are disorganized.
- You don't like schedules.
- You are not concerned with health, diet, fitness, or commitment.
- You live for the moment.

AFTER SAUL'S (AKA Paul's) supernatural encounter and conversion to Christ, he quickly fled from Damascus because of the great persecution and suspicion coming from both the disciples and the religious leaders. (See Acts 9:20–25.) Paul then spent the next three years in Nabataean Arabia (modern-day Turkey) being discipled by the revelation of Christ Himself. (See Galatians 1:11–12, 15–18.)

Some people think that God gave Paul three years of one-on-one teaching because the original twelve disciples had three years with Jesus. Paul showed great personal discipline in waiting on Christ to release him for his teaching ministry. Being disciplined is a characteristic that mature believers possess.

SCRIPTURE PASSAGES

The apostle Paul demonstrated remarkable discipline in the face of all kinds of resistance and opposition. As you read these texts, reflect on the ways God might use your fast to cultivate the same kind of discipline you see on display here.

> As he went he drew near Damascus, and suddenly a light from heaven shone around him. He fell to the ground and heard a voice saying to him, "Saul, Saul, why do you persecute Me?"
>
> He said, "Who are You, Lord?"
>
> The Lord said, "I am Jesus, whom you are persecuting. It is hard for you to kick against the goads."...
>
> Immediately something like scales fell from his eyes, and he could see again. And he rose up and was baptized. When he had eaten, he was strengthened.
>
> For several days Saul was with the disciples in Damascus. Immediately he preached in the synagogues that the Christ is the Son of God. All who heard him were amazed and said, "Is not this he who killed those who called on this name in Jerusalem, and came here with that intent, to bring them bound to the chief priests?" Yet Saul increased all the more with power and confounded the Jews living in Damascus, proving that this One is the Christ.
>
> After many days had passed, the Jews arranged to kill him. But their scheme was known by Saul. They watched the gates day and night to kill him. But the disciples took him by night, and lowered him in a basket through the wall.
>
> When Saul had come to Jerusalem, he tried to join the disciples. But they all feared him, not believing he was a disciple. But Barnabas took him, and led him to the apostles, and declared to them how on the road he had seen the Lord, and that He had spoken to him, and how he had boldly preached in Damascus in the name of Jesus. So he stayed with them while coming in and going out of Jerusalem. And he spoke boldly in the name of the Lord Jesus and disputed against the Hellenists. But they tried to kill him. When the brothers learned this, they brought him down to Caesarea, and sent him off to Tarsus.
>
> —ACTS 9:3–5, 18–30, MEV

But I reveal to you, brothers, that the gospel which was preached by me is not according to man. For I neither received it from man, neither was I taught it, except by a revelation of Jesus Christ.

For you have heard of my former life in Judaism, how I persecuted the church of God beyond measure and tried to destroy it, and progressed in Judaism above many of my equals in my own heritage, being more exceedingly zealous for the traditions of my fathers. But when it pleased God, who set me apart since I was in my mother's womb and called me by His grace, to reveal His Son in me, that I might preach Him among the nations, I did not immediately confer with flesh and blood, nor did I go up to Jerusalem to those who were apostles before me. But I went into Arabia, and returned again to Damascus. After three years I went up to Jerusalem to see Peter and stayed with him for fifteen days.

—GALATIANS 1:11–18, MEV

GOING DEEPER

The apostle Paul was born in the city of Tarsus to an Israelite family of the tribe of Benjamin (Phil. 3:5). His parents, who were followers of Judaism, had him circumcised on the eighth day according to the law of God (Gen. 17:12). Being very zealous for God, they sent him to Jerusalem to be taught by the Pharisees and leading rabbis. The school was led by the well-respected Rabbi Gamaliel, who personally taught the future apostle (Acts 5:34; 22:3).

So, we can see from his childhood that Saul was taught to be disciplined and zealous for God. The growing movement of Jesus was causing quite a ruckus. Saul thought it his duty to stop the coming revolution and wipe out the Way of Christianity—but God had a different plan for him. As we read in our passage today, God struck him blind and then spoke one on one to the soon-to-be new convert of Christ. Saul knew he was encountering someone beyond natural understanding—he was encountering the risen Jesus.

Paul determined that he could not stay where he was and fled to Arabia for safety. It is there that the revelation of Christ personally taught him the fundamentals of Jesus—the Way, the Truth, and the Life. The practice of self-discipline and hard study served him well as he relearned the law of God.

Discipline is not taught in our homes and schools today as it once was. Hard work, focus, and challenges are now thought to be burdensome and have gone the way of our parents' teaching and "old-school" thinking. It is sad that children are given trophies and awards for just showing up and not for the hard work and discipline we used to value. College test requirements have been reduced to accommodate all students. While I am all for finding creative ways to assist students, we cannot lower our standards or make excuses for not holding the bar high. School did not come easy for me, but my parents, teachers, and good old hard work all helped teach me discipline and eventually contributed to the success I have today.

Scripture is very clear on the matter of discipline. Proverbs 12:1 says, "Whoever loves instruction loves knowledge, but he who hates correction is stupid." Proverbs 15:5 says, "A fool despises his father's instruction, but he who receives correction is prudent." Proverbs consistently demonstrates that instruction and self-discipline bring wisdom and knowledge.

Discipline does not come naturally for most people. We must train and equip ourselves for the outcome we wish to attain. Whether it be physical results, mental breakthroughs, or spiritual growth, it all takes self-discipline.

I love the story of the conversion of the apostle Paul. He was converted not only spiritually but also mentally and emotionally. As we know, Paul was already trained in academia in the ways of Judaism, but now he was being challenged to rethink his conviction and to receive a new message, a new way of understanding. This took courage and discipline and willingness to receive instruction from the Spirit of God. His instruction while in Arabia was just the beginning of his life journey. He would go on to be beaten, persecuted, tempted, and tried, yet through it all he remained faithful. That is the test of self-discipline: Are you faithful to your commitment?

> Discipline does not come naturally for most people. We must train and equip ourselves for the outcome we wish to attain.

Paul's testimony to his young protégé, Timothy, was, "I have fought the good fight, I have finished the race, I have kept the faith" (2 Tim. 4:7). Only discipline will prove the test of time. Our testimony is the most powerful tool we have to share with others. Make sure you are living a life worthy of those watching.

FOR FURTHER STUDY

One of the great blessings of a fast is the way this one discipline tends to sharpen and refine our discipline in every arena of life. The following verses highlight the importance of discipline. Read them with an open heart and look for the ways God wants to bring you into the kind of deeper discipline that ushers in change.

- Proverbs 12:1

- Job 5:17

- 1 Corinthians 9:27

- Proverbs 3:11–12

- Proverbs 15:5

- Proverbs 1:7

- 1 Peter 1:13

COACHING STEPS

1. First, you must understand that self-discipline is a battle you and only you can fight. You must want change more than you don't. Hard work, accountability, and strategies will bring about the results you desire. Take a moment right now and make a list of areas in which you need personal discipline—is it fitness, health, work, or spiritual growth? Until you can see your outcome, you will never follow through. What does discipline look like for you in each of these areas?

2. Next, take consistent small steps. What are the steps you need to take to move forward? Identify where you want to grow. Now, what are two or three steps you can take in each area? This might mean recruiting someone to hold you accountable, or setting boundaries and personal standards for yourself. I have found that my clients who set clear goals for themselves are the ones who achieve the results they long for.

3. Stop making excuses. You picked up this book because you want some sort of change in your life—and change takes work. Most of us love the idea of new goals and future dreams, but the truth is, most of the time, that is all they are—thoughts. You must erase the excuses. That means you no longer give yourself permission to fail. You are committed and focused on the outcome of your decision. Take some time now and write down the things that are keeping you undisciplined: laziness, busyness, being unsure about how to proceed, or justifying your lifestyle, to name a few. After you write them down, cross through them with a yellow highlighter. Next to your excuses, write two or three action steps you will take to practice self-discipline and the follow-through actions you will take. You are the only one who can make yourself do this. The question is, Do you want the characteristic of discipline in your life or not?

THE JESUS FAST

We have no greater example of self-discipline than our Lord and Savior, Jesus Christ. In the wilderness, while fasting for forty days, Jesus battled the greatest temptation and evil known to man embodied in a physical manifestation of Satan himself. Yet Jesus was victorious and an overcomer. Why? Because He chose to yield to the power of a living God.

Jesus, being fully God yet fully man, had the same temptations and opportunities we have—to walk in the fullness of the Spirit, or to walk in our own plans and dreams. Satan provided every opportunity for Jesus to succumb to temptation, but our Lord knew the consequences of following the plans of Satan. Instead, He used the

Word of God to battle each offer of the enemy. Discipline takes will-power and determination. On your fast today, ask God to give you the strength to overcome the evil one, to help you make the right choices, and to say no to the enemy's voice in your life. Practice self-discipline and see how God blesses your day and brings you undeniable joy.

DISCUSSION QUESTIONS

- Today we looked at the life of the apostle Paul. We learned that although he was educated at the finest synagogues in Damascus, he was misinformed. Many people today follow false teaching and legalistic leaders, but Jesus has come to set us free. Paul sat for three years learning the teachings of Jesus. Have you ever sat quietly and allowed Jesus to speak with you, to teach you something new and fresh from His Word? If not, take a moment right now and sit alone with Jesus. What did He say to you?

- The life we choose to live is on us. God gives us the freedom to choose life or death, salvation in His Son or the rejection of His love. You also have the choice between a life of discipline or laziness. We cannot blame others for where we are today. Take a moment and reevaluate your life journey. Do you need to make any course corrections? If so, what would that look like?

- Jesus battled Satan in the wilderness by using the Word of God. Often we don't know how to do warfare with the enemy because we do not know

Scripture. What are your greatest weaknesses—fear, anger, anxiety, loneliness, pride? Take some time today to locate three or four scriptures that give you strength over your weakness. You can use your cross reference found in the back of your Bible or, of course, google Scripture references. Write down these verses in your journal entry for today. Now rehearse these verses each day until they become part of your daily conversation.

PRAYER

Dear Lord, I realized today that I have areas in my life in which I am undisciplined. I agree with You that I need to make a change. I ask that You give me the power and fortitude to stay committed and determined to see my way through excuses and laziness. Lord, I want to walk with You in power and obedience. In Jesus' name, amen.

JOURNAL ENTRY

_____

_____

_____

_____

_____

day
17

FASTING FOR
WONDER

THE QUEEN OF SHEBA

Let anyone laugh and taunt if he so wishes. I am not keeping silent, nor am I hiding the signs and wonders that were shown to me by the Lord many years before they happened, who knew everything, even before the beginning of time.

—SAINT PATRICK

won·der | ˈwən-dər |

verb

desire or be curious to know something

SIGNS OF LACK OF WONDER

- You don't have an interest in what you don't know.
- You look at life as routine and predictable.
- You don't like change.
- You don't go out of your way to learn new things.
- You are suspicious of others.

WONDER IS A word we don't use much today. I fear we have become so wise in our own eyes that we don't pursue the deep things of God. Yet in our story today we will find a woman, a queen, who would push past all obstacles to personally seek out the wonder and wisdom of King Solomon. I love that the queen went on the journey for herself. She could have sent her servants or advisors—but no, she traveled herself. She wanted to find the answers to her own deepest longings, her own deepest questions. No one can do the work for you. You, too, must seek and find the truth for yourself.

SCRIPTURE PASSAGE

You may not be a queen or a king, but the tenacity of this queen shows us how wonder, astonishment, and willingness to ask hard questions can take us wherever we need to go. As you read her story, contemplate what characteristics she embodies that you may need to pick up on your own journey.

Now when the queen of Sheba heard of Solomon's fame connected to the name of the LORD, she came to test him with hard questions. She came to Jerusalem with a very great retinue, with camels bearing spices, and very much gold, and precious stones; and when she came to Solomon, she told him all that was on her mind. Solomon answered all her questions; there was not anything too difficult for the king which he could not answer. When the queen of Sheba observed Solomon's wisdom and the house he had built and the meat of his table and the sitting of his servants and the attendance of his ministers and their clothing and his cupbearers and his entryway by which he went up to the house of the LORD, it took her breath away.

She said to the king, "What I heard in my own land about your acts and your wisdom was true! I did not believe it until I came and saw it with my own eyes! In fact, I was not even told half. Your wisdom and prosperity are greater than the stories I heard! Happy are your men, and happy are these your servants who stand continually before you and hear your wisdom! Blessed be the LORD your God, who delighted in you and set you on the throne of Israel, because the LORD loved Israel forever; therefore He made you king in order to execute judgment and justice."

She gave the king a hundred and twenty talents of gold and a great amount of spices and precious stones. No one gave as many spices as the queen of Sheba gave to King Solomon.

The ships of Hiram, which brought gold from Ophir, also brought from Ophir a large quantity of almug wood and precious stones. The king made pillars for the house of the LORD out of the almug trees and harps also and psalteries for singers for the king's house. Never before had such almug wood been brought, nor has any such been seen to this day.

King Solomon gave to the queen of Sheba all she desired, no matter what she asked for, in addition to what Solomon gave her from his royal bounty. So she turned and went to her own country, she and her servants.

—1 KINGS 10:1–13, MEV

GOING DEEPER

The Queen of Sheba had everything a woman could want—beauty, fame, wealth, and a kingdom—but she still desired more. She longed for connection and meaning. Word had begun to spread about the wisdom of King Solomon, of his God, his knowledge, and his leadership. She had a hunger and a wonder that led her on the journey to sit with Solomon and learn from his teachings. This journey was estimated to be three years long. She traveled roughly 1,500 miles to sit face to face with this king. Along with her she brought camels, spices, gold, and precious stones as a gift to impress him.

The queen asked Solomon many difficult questions and grilled him with great intrigue. It is not until you are fully willing to sacrifice it all that you will ever see the wonder of what God has for you. It's easy to lose our wonder in the self-sufficient society we live in today. We presume we know enough about life and God, and even our personal desires, but most of us sell ourselves short by not risking it all to gaze into the wonder of our almighty God. If we will let it, wonder will lead us deeper and grow our faith and maturity.

In Habakkuk 1:5 the Bible says, "Look among the nations, and see; wonder and be astounded. For I am doing a work in your days that you would not believe if told" (ESV). Look at that phrase "wonder and be astounded." When was the last time you were astounded?

People are ripe to experience wonder again. I believe we are living in a time of revival. The three years of the pandemic caused the church to wake up and say, "No more!" We are once again asking God for healing and hope in our land. We are seeing breakouts of confession and repentance. When that happens, God moves. This provokes the awe and wonder of God. God is still doing works we would not believe even if we were told. Never stop wondering.

I remember many years ago going away for an overnight fasting retreat. It was just God and I in the mountains of Colorado at a Christian retreat center. I remember going outside that night and sitting wrapped in a blanket in front of a fire and looking up at the stars. I was completely astonished. It happened to be one of those beautiful, clear nights when it seems as though every star that God created is dancing in glory. I remember tearing up with emotion at the beauty of God's creation. When we get alone with God and have intimate experiences with the Holy Spirit, it takes our wonder to a level of astonishment.

You must have this desire, a longing in your soul to know that there is more out there for you to see.

FOR FURTHER STUDY

Let the words of these scriptures stoke your sense of wonder and astonishment today.

- Luke 5:26

- Exodus 15:11

- Psalm 33:8

- Exodus 3:20

- Deuteronomy 1:30

- 1 Chronicles 16:24

- Job 11:6

- Psalm 26:7

COACHING STEPS

1. The most important step in building a desire for wonder is to believe there is *more for you*. We are ever growing in the knowledge of ourselves and of God. Begin by asking God to show you what He has for your future. Dream again, and allow your mind to explore the depths of God's goodness. This opens the doorway for you to see things from a new perspective.

2. Seek out those who can encourage and build your faith. The Queen of Sheba sought out the wisdom of God. Don't wait for someone to come to you; go looking for knowledge and wisdom. Allow your wonder to grow. Ask hard questions, and be honest and not afraid to seek the answers.

3. Get vulnerable. Now, that may seem odd or even hard for you to understand, but it is not until you lower your guard and defense mechanisms that you ever honestly see the pure wonder of God. The wonder of God is a mystery that goes beyond our mind's capacity to comprehend, but when we step into our childlike faith, we can begin to dream and believe again.

THE JESUS FAST

Not only did Jesus fast for forty days in the wilderness, but He also told His disciples to fast. He taught them that some things in our lives only happen by prayer and fasting. He taught them how to take authority over all principalities and powers that try to come up against them. He taught them about demonic forces that need to be called out and rebuked in the name of Jesus (Matt. 17:21). While on your fast today, take time to remember the power Jesus has given you to walk in authority. Enjoy the awe and wonder of God leading you step by step on the journey of life.

DISCUSSION QUESTIONS

- Have you ever been attracted to someone for their wisdom and leadership? You knew there was something special about them, and you wanted to know more. That is called wonder. Take a moment and write down what it was that made you notice them. It was obviously something you liked. What are a few things in your life that you would like to develop and take to a higher level?

- The Queen of Sheba thought she could impress King Solomon with her wealth, but his wisdom was neither for sale nor something she could acquire on her own. True wisdom comes from the heart of God. Her wonder led her to his wisdom. That is how it works: we seek out the things of God because we desire them. Do you have wonder and curiosity to go deeper with God, to follow far and wide to find the wisdom of God? Take some time now and evaluate your heart. Only you know what is next on your path with Him. Write your response below.

- We read that the queen had many difficult questions for King Solomon, and he was ready to answer them. She came and tested him with hard questions. If someone were to ask you to explain your spiritual journey, would you be able to answer? There are two takeaways from our passage today: First, allow the wisdom of God to flow through your life so that others want what you have. Second, be ready and equipped to share the story of God's wisdom and blessings in your life.

PRAYER

Dear Lord, I desire to go deeper in my awe and wonder of Your goodness. I ask that You fill me with Your Spirit and lead me. Teach me how to stop and see Your wonder and majesty in my everyday life. Lord, I ask You to help me share my journey with those around me and be spiritually attractive to those whom I encounter. In Jesus' name, amen.

JOURNAL ENTRY

_____

_____

_____

_____

_____

day
18

FASTING FOR
COMPASSION

THE WOMEN WHO WASHED JESUS' FEET

Compassion will cure more sins than condemnation.

—HENRY WARD BEECHER

Man may dismiss compassion from his heart,
but God never will.

—WILLIAM COWPER

com·pas·sion | kəm-ˈpa-shən |

noun

sympathetic pity and concern for the sufferings or misfortunes of others

SIGNS OF LACK OF COMPASSION

- You think you deserve more because you work harder.
- You drive right by the needs of others.
- You judge those in need.
- You are selfish.
- You justify that you helped someone in the past, and they just returned to their old ways.

Compassion is woven throughout Scripture. Whether it be the love of a father waiting patiently for his prodigal son to return home, sweet Dorcas caring for the poor and widows in the Book of Acts, or the kind deeds of Boaz, who provided food for the gleaners to gather in the fields, the Bible contains story after story of compassionate hearts that cared for the well-being of others. But the greatest example of compassion we read about is the love and sacrifice of our Lord and Savior. Psalm 86:15 says, "But You, O Lord, are a God full of compassion, and gracious, longsuffering and abundant in mercy and truth." Today we will see that compassion can be experienced in both giving and receiving.

SCRIPTURE PASSAGES

The ultimate goal of fasting is not just to shape our hearts toward God, but to reorient our hearts toward others. Jesus is the perfect exemplar of many things, but perhaps most of all, compassion. As we enter the stories of the following two women, observe the compassion of Jesus, and read prayerfully, open for God to show you the ways you need to practice this compassion in your own life.

> One of the Pharisees asked Him to eat with him. So He went to the Pharisee's house and sat down for supper. There, a woman of the city who was a sinner, when she learned that Jesus was sitting for supper in the Pharisee's house, brought an alabaster jar of ointment, and stood behind Him at His feet, weeping, and began to wash His feet with tears, and wiped them with the hair of her head, and kissed His feet, and anointed them with the ointment.
>
> Now when the Pharisee who had invited Him saw it, he said to himself, "If this Man were a prophet, He would have known who and what kind of woman she is who is touching Him, for she is a sinner."…
>
> Then He turned to the woman and said to Simon, "Do you see this woman? I entered your house. You gave Me no water for My feet, but she has washed My feet with her tears and wiped them with the hair of her head. You gave Me no kiss, but this woman, since the time I came in, has not ceased to kiss My feet. You did not anoint My head with oil, but this woman has anointed My feet with ointment. Therefore I say to you, her sins, which are many, are forgiven, for she loved much. But he who is forgiven little loves little."
>
> Then He said to her, "Your sins are forgiven."
>
> Those who sat at supper with Him began to say to themselves, "Who is He who even forgives sins?"
>
> He said to the woman, "Your faith has saved you. Go in peace."
>
> —LUKE 7:36–39, 44–50, MEV

Six days before the Passover Jesus came to Bethany, where Lazarus was, who had been dead, whom He had raised from the dead. They prepared a supper for Him there. Martha served, but Lazarus was one of those who sat at the table with Him. Then Mary took a pint of very costly ointment made from pure nard, and anointed the feet of Jesus, and wiped His feet with her hair. The house was filled with the fragrance of the ointment.

But one of His disciples, Judas Iscariot, Simon's son, who would betray Him, said, "Why was this ointment not sold for three hundred denarii and given to the poor?" He said this, not because he cared for the poor, but because he was a thief. And having the money box, he used to steal what was put in it.

But Jesus said, "Leave her alone. She has kept this for the day of My burial."

—JOHN 12:1–7, MEV

GOING DEEPER

Compassion is a two-way street: our compassion toward others, and others' compassion toward us. In the Bible we find the stories of two distinct women, both named Mary, both of whom wiped the feet of Jesus for two completely different reasons. The first Mary was being ridiculed and belittled for her past life, a life of prostitution. She was persecuted and rejected because of her former life. Jesus boldly stood up to the Pharisee Simon and reminded him publicly that Mary gave Him something to drink, that she anointed His head with oil, and that she wiped His feet with her tears, while Simon himself did nothing as he welcomed Jesus into his home.

It was a tradition in Judaism to wash the feet of a guest coming in from the dirt road and welcome them in. To anoint Jesus was to recognize that He was who He said He was. When Jesus spoke to Simon, He did so in a way that entailed public humiliation, yet He spoke with compassion toward Mary. He elevated Mary, and He humbled Simon.

Then we have the story of another Mary—the sister of Martha and Lazarus—overwhelmed by the goodness and graciousness of Jesus. Knowing her time with Him was short, she had deep compassion and reverence toward her Lord. She washed His feet with her hair as her emotional tears fell upon Him. She showed deep compassion toward Jesus.

I'm sure Mary had not forgotten when Jesus miraculously raised her brother, Lazarus, from the dead, or the great pearls of wisdom Jesus taught her as she sat at His feet while Martha busied herself with chores. I believe she intuitively knew Jesus would not be with them long. Honor and love came rushing out of her heart as she fell prostrate at His feet. Compassion will overwhelm your soul and humble your heart.

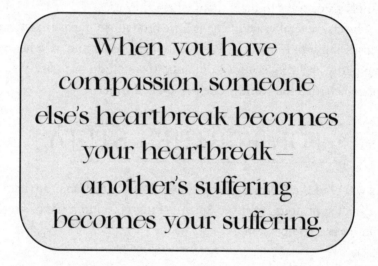

When you have compassion, someone else's heartbreak becomes your heartbreak — another's suffering becomes your suffering.

Two different Marys, two different stories, yet the same characteristic: *compassion*.

In the first story we see the compassion Jesus had for a broken woman. He brought honor to her name as a reflection of her heart. Humbled yet full of joy, she bowed in reverence and respect at the feet of Jesus to give all she had to the only One who truly saw her.

The root word helps us understand the true heart and meaning of compassion. In Latin, *compati* means "to suffer with." When you have compassion, someone else's heartbreak becomes your heartbreak—another's suffering becomes your suffering.

I have had to examine my heart lately with regard to my own capacity for compassion. In my daily work, I see more and more people needing assistance and resources. I see homeless and broken refugees on an everyday basis. It is easy to think they should just get a job or find a means of income, but compassion leads us to see them as people. My daughter is the missions pastor at Influence Church and has taught me a great deal about the heart of compassion. She never complains or gossips about those in need. She simply finds ways to meet them where they are.

The last several years of chaos have brought so much anxiety and depression into our world. We need more people to have a heart of sympathy and concern for humanity. If we all do our part, we can indeed change the world—one person at a time.

FOR FURTHER STUDY

As you read the following scriptures, allow yourself to hear them as a direct summons from the Spirit calling you into a life of greater and deeper compassion.

- Ephesians 4:32
- Lamentations 3:22–23
- 1 Peter 3:8
- Zechariah 7:9–10
- Micah 7:19
- Isaiah 30:18

COACHING STEPS

1. The first step in developing compassion is seeing others as equals. It is so easy to judge and ridicule those who don't look like us or act like us. Our culture, training, and convictions all play a role in who we are today. Some of us have been fortunate to have healthy homes and encouraging families, but this is not the case for everyone. When you pass someone in need, ask yourself, "Is there something I can do to help?" If your first response is unkind, you probably need to help them out.

2. We have all been in situations where someone has been belittled or demeaned. Our response should always be to speak up and stop the hateful conversation. We can teach others how to respect one another simply by taking control of the conversation. Just as Jesus did to both Simon and Judas, we too can speak up on behalf of others.

3. Another important tool that helps us develop compassion is the art of forgiveness. Most of us hold on to the things others have done to hurt or embarrass us. We reason that we have the right to be angry and resentful, but the truth is that unforgiveness only hurts us. When we choose to forgive and forget, we not only show compassion to those involved but we also set ourselves free from heartache and pain. Whom do you need to forgive today? Are you ready to exercise compassion?

THE JESUS FAST

There is not a more compassionate person that walked this earth than Jesus. As we read the passage in Matthew 4 about Jesus fasting in the wilderness, we can only imagine the human struggle He encountered for us—not just going without food, but also the constant attack from Satan reminding Him of the reason He came for humanity. Do you think Jesus ever asked Himself why He was doing this? Why give Himself sacrificially for a group of people that would turn their backs on Him?

A person with compassion acts out of love and not anger. Jesus was the perfect Son of God who came to earth to redeem His children—that is what grace and goodness look like. While on your fast today, ask yourself these questions: Have I thanked Jesus lately for what He did for me on the cross? Have I gone out of my way to help someone less fortunate? And lastly, would you say you have a heart of compassion for others?

DISCUSSION QUESTIONS

- In today's study we read about two very different women, both named Mary. One experienced the compassion of Jesus, while the other gave compassion to Jesus. Do you think you give or receive more compassion? Are you meeting the needs of others, or are you receiving assistance and appreciation from those around you? On the lines below, take a moment and write down the names of people you have helped or shown compassion to recently.

- When you see a homeless or needy person on the street, what is your first thought? Is it sorrow? Judgment? From today's lesson, will you be more apt to see the needs of those around you? What are some steps you can take to meet the needs of others? A few suggestions are to volunteer at local shelters or your church missions department, keep cash in your car to help those in need, make grocery bags of nonperishable foods to keep in your car, or sponsor a child in need. There are so many ways we can show compassion to others in our communities.

- Are you part of the problem, or part of the solution? Do you make fun of those who are less fortunate, or are you their advocate? What would you say to someone who was belittling or condemning another human being? Would you ignore it, or would you speak up? It is important that we see others the way God sees them—as valuable and worthy of love. How would you handle a conversation that was inappropriate and unkind? Share your thoughts below.

PRAYER

Dear Lord, I confess that I have not always had a heart of compassion. I admit that I have judged or overlooked those around me in need. Lord, I ask that You forgive me. I ask that You teach me to see others with the heart of compassion that You have. I want to have grace and patience for those who need my support. Today I commit to starting fresh and having the image of humanity that You desire. In Jesus' name, amen.

JOURNAL ENTRY

_____

_____

_____

_____

_____

_____

_____

_____

_____

_____

_____

_____

_____

_____

day
19

FASTING FOR
SELF-CONTROL

— ABIGAIL —

We must have a spirit of power towards the enemy,

a spirit of love towards men, and a spirit of

self-control towards ourselves.

—WATCHMAN NEE

self-con·trol | ˌself-kən-ˈtrōl |

noun

the ability to control oneself, in particular one's emotions and desires or the expression of them in one's behavior, especially in difficult situations

SIGNS OF LACK OF SELF-CONTROL

- You seek to meet your needs above the needs of others.
- You don't have boundaries or discipline.
- You are triggered by your emotions.
- You don't do well under pressure.
- You are prideful.

SELF-CONTROL ALWAYS PAYS off. In our story today we find a woman who acted with insight and wisdom to stop what could have been a brutal annihilation of her servants. Abigail was a beautiful, God-fearing woman who made haste in repairing a situation her prideful husband had created. Self-control comes by choosing to make the best decisions, which are not always the easiest ones. Our own personal desires and interests often keep us from living lives of self-control.

Today we will see that God goes before those who seek His ways and counsel. Often our tendency is to react out of anger or pride, thinking our way is best. But when we slow down long enough to think through the process, we discover that, with a little patience and counsel, we may need to change our course. This is what self-control is all about: thinking before reacting.

SCRIPTURE PASSAGE

Today's passage vividly illustrates the power of self-control—both when it is harnessed, as it was for the brilliant Abigail, and when this virtue is ignored, as it was by her corrupt husband, Nabal. As you read this story, reflect on the ways God may be using your fast to call you to exercise greater self-control.

Now there was a man in Maon whose work was in Carmel. He was a rich man with three thousand sheep and a thousand goats, and he was shearing his sheep in Carmel. The man's name was Nabal and the name of his wife Abigail. She was a woman of good understanding and beautiful, but the man was harsh and evil in his actions and he was a Calebite.

David heard in the wilderness that Nabal was shearing his sheep. So David sent out ten young men, and David said to the young men, "Go up to Carmel, and go to Nabal and greet him in my name. And thus you will you say to him who lives in prosperity, 'Peace be to you and peace to your house, and to all that you have, peace.

"'I have heard that you have shearers. Now your shepherds were with us. We did not harm them nor did they miss anything all the days they were in Carmel. Ask your young men and they will tell you. Therefore let my young men find favor in your eyes, for we have come on a good day. Please give whatever you find at hand to your servants, and to your son David.'"

When David's young men came, they spoke to Nabal according to all these words in the name of David, then they waited.

And Nabal answered David's servants, and said, "Who is David? And who is the son of Jesse? Today many servants are breaking away each one from his master. Should I then take my bread, and my water, and my meat, that which I have killed for my shearers, and give it to men whose origins are unknown?"

So David's young men turned themselves around and went back. And they came and reported to him all these words. David said to his men, "Each man strap on his sword." And each man strapped on his sword. David also put on his sword, and four hundred men went up after David. But two hundred stayed with the baggage.

Now one of the young men told Abigail, Nabal's wife, "Listen, David sent messengers out of the wilderness to bless our master; and he railed against them. But the men were very good to us, and we were not harmed, nor did we miss anything, all the days we went about with them in the field. They were a wall to us both by night and day, all the days we were with them keeping the flocks. Now therefore know and consider what you will do, for evil is determined against our master and against all his household. He is such a worthless man that one cannot speak to him."

Then Abigail hurried and took two hundred loaves, two bottles of wine, five prepared sheep, five measures of roasted grain, a hundred clusters of raisins, and two hundred cakes of figs, and she loaded them on donkeys. And she said to her servants, "Go on before me. See, I will be coming after you." But she did not tell her husband Nabal.

And as she was riding on the donkey and going down into the cover of the mountain, David and his men were coming down to meet her and she met them. Now David had said, "Surely in vain have I guarded all that this man has in the wilderness, so that nothing was missed of all that belonged to him. And he has returned me evil for good. So may God do unto the enemies of David and more also, if by morning I leave even one male of all who belong to him."

When Abigail saw David, she hurriedly got down from the donkey and fell before David upon her face. And she bowed herself to the ground. So she fell at his feet and said, "Against me alone, my lord, is the guilt. Please let your handmaid speak in your ears, and hear the words of your handmaid. Please do not let my lord set his heart against this worth-less man, against Nabal. For as his name is, so is he. Nabal is his name and folly is with him. But I, your handmaid, did not see the young men of my lord, whom you sent. Now my lord, as the LORD lives, and as your soul lives, because the LORD has restrained you from coming in bloodshed and from avenging yourself with your own hand, now let your enemies, and those seeking to do evil to my lord, be as Nabal. Now let this blessing which your maidservant has brought to my lord be given to the young men who follow my lord.

"Please forgive the transgression of your handmaid, for the LORD will certainly make my lord a sure house, because my lord fights the battles of the LORD, and evil will not be found in you all your days. Even if a man rises to pursue you and to seek your life, the life of my lord will be bound in the bundle of the living with the LORD your God. But the lives of your enemies He will sling out, as from the hollow of a sling. It will be, when the LORD does for my lord according to all the good that He has spoken concerning you and has appointed you ruler over Israel, that this will be no grief to you, nor an offense of heart to my lord, either that you have shed blood without cause, or that my lord has avenged himself. But when the LORD has dealt well with my lord, then remember your handmaid."

David said to Abigail, "Blessed be the LORD, God of Israel, who sent you this day to meet me. And blessed is your dis-cretion, and blessed are you who have kept me this day from coming to shed blood and from avenging myself with my own hand. For as the LORD, the God of Israel lives, who has restrained me from injuring you, if you had not hurried to come and meet me, surely there would not have been left even one male to Nabal by the morning light."

So David received from her hand what she had brought him and said to her, "Go up in peace to your house. See, I have obeyed your voice, and have granted your request."

Abigail came to Nabal, and he was feasting in his house, like the feast of a king. And Nabal's heart was merry within him, for he was very drunk. Therefore she told him nothing until the morning light. But in the morning when the wine was gone out of Nabal, his wife told him these things. And his heart died within him, and he became as a stone. And about ten days after that, the LORD struck Nabal and he died.

When David heard that Nabal was dead, he said, "Blessed is the LORD, who has defended the cause of my reproach from the hand of Nabal, and has kept His servant from evil. For the LORD has returned the wickedness of Nabal upon his own head."

And David sent and spoke with Abigail, to take her as his wife. When the servants of David came to Abigail at Carmel, they spoke to her, saying, "David has sent us to you to take you as his wife."

—1 SAMUEL 25:2–40, MEV

GOING DEEPER

What a beautifully scripted story. We have the selfish and entitled husband, the beautiful and wise wife, the desperate servants, and the powerful-yet-humble soon-to-be king. Self-control played a part in each of these characters' stories. Some used it to their benefit, and others ignored it.

Our story opens with the introduction of Nabal, a harsh and evil man, along with his wife, Abigail, a woman with wisdom and understanding who was also beautiful. As the events unfold, we learn that David sent word to Nabal that he and his men were in their area, asking that he would provide for them. He informed Nabal that David and his men had been kind to Nabal's shepherds while they were far from home, and that he was requesting assistance in return.

This was a reasonable request; the problem was that it was sent to an unreasonable man. Pride and arrogance filled Nabal's heart, and he sent word back that under no circumstances would he send aid to David. Feeling quite empowered, Nabal threw a feast for himself and became intoxicated. Meanwhile, his wife, Abigail, took matters into her hands and went to work to save their household.

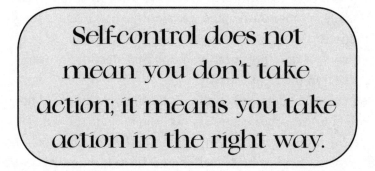

Self-control does not mean you don't take action; it means you take action in the right way.

Scripture is clear to say that David was a man in power and that he gave complete respect and honor to Nabal and his men. But the line had been drawn, and David could no longer tolerate such disrespect. He charged his soldiers to saddle up, and four hundred men took off to do battle with naughty Nabal.

Fortunately, upon hearing what had transpired, Abigail made haste and prepared food and supplies for David and his men. Quickly she sent her servants before her to lead the way, as she loaded her donkey and followed behind. As she approached David, with honor Abigail bowed low and began to ask for forgiveness for her husband. She offered him bread, wine, raisins, and grain. "Please, my lord, do not bring injustice upon our household because of the foolishness of my husband." David was taken aback by her boldness and control. This was a woman worth listening to.

Self-control will always get the attention of others. It is both attractive and inspiring. David did indeed hear the words of Abigail, and he spared Nabal's household—but God was not finished with the story.

Abigail waited until Nabal was sober the next morning to recount the foolishness of his actions. Timing is an important key to self-control. Upon learning of his rash behavior, Nabal was filled with fear and immediately fell over like stone. The actions resulting from a lack of self-control will absolutely rob you of life. This man lost his life because of the poor decisions he had made throughout his lifetime.

Self-control does not mean you don't take action; it means you take action in the right way.

Self-control understands timing. Abigail knew she could not wait for Nabal to get sober before she did something. She did not seek his permission or advice before going to David. She made haste and prepared food as he requested and then, in humility and confidence, approached him with forgiveness. This courageous act did not go unnoticed by David or by Abigail's servants.

As we conclude the story, we find that after Nabal's death, David sent word that he would like to marry Abigail. It is the perfect love story—two people with similar responses toward the well-being of others always seem to find each other.

Self-control comes in many forms. Personal discipline, focus, conviction, well-being, and goals all fall under the category of self-control. Self-control allows you to alter your responses so you avoid undesirable behaviors while instead developing desirable ones. It also aids you in achieving long-term goals.

Examples of self-control include things like monitoring your social media so it doesn't affect your productivity, having the discipline to not purchase something you want because you are trying to stick to a budget, and avoiding sweets because you are trying to reduce your sugar intake. But I think one of the biggest ways to practice self-control is to manage and control your emotional responses—for example, walking away when someone does something that makes you feel angry or upset.

As with Nabal, some people struggle with self-control because of pride and arrogance. Their tempers and emotions rule their reactions, and before long they just can't hold their responses. The Bible teaches us in Galatians 5:22–23 that the fruit of the Spirit of God is "love, joy, peace, longsuffering, kindness, goodness, faithfulness, gentleness, self-control." When we are filled with the Holy Spirit of God, we can walk in self-control. The question is, Are we willing to yield to the Spirit of God and allow our fleshly actions to die? The real battle is fought over our will; will we yield to God or go our own way?

FOR FURTHER STUDY

All of the following passages summon us to the kind of self-control that marks a person who walks in the Spirit. One of the great benefits of fasting is that God uses it to develop self-control in us. As you read these words, reflect on the ways God may be inviting you to a greater exercise of self-control—not so He can dominate you, but to bring you into a life in which you are no longer dominated.

- Galatians 5:22–23
- Proverbs 29:11
- Psalm 141:3–4
- James 1:19
- Isaiah 53:7
- Proverbs 18:6–7
- Proverbs 13:3

COACHING STEPS

1. Wanting to make a change is not enough to bring about change. We live in a self-gratifying culture where people are prone to seek their own desires before the desires of others. Change requires discipline and self-control. If you truly want to grow in your personal life, you must have a plan to get where you want to go. Putting in the work and making an effort is what brings about the results. Begin to identify two or three areas in which you need to exercise self-control—physical exercise, food consumption, social media, your conversations about others, and so on. Now, write those down. What steps can you take to make a difference in these areas? Write down the steps you will take to start seeing more self-control—things like personal accountability, changing the environment you are currently in, or maybe praying and asking God to help you. You must know where you want to go before you can take the steps to get there.

2. Stop making excuses for yourself like, "It's just who I am," "I don't know what to do," or "I don't have anyone to help me." Excuses are nothing more than endless air that will keep you stuck and discouraged. Admit to yourself that you can do this. You *can* make a change. Yes, it will take work, accountability, and most of all, God, but you can develop the traits and characteristics you desire. Begin to see yourself growing and developing into *more*—more of who God created you to be. Now, write down a

declaration sentence explaining where you see yourself one year from today. The power of our words and vision will pave the way for our destiny.

3. We have talked a lot about accountability. That's because it is the key to your success. Think of someone you admire and respect. What is it about them that stands out? Typically they are things like faithfulness, reliability, and personal success. Did you know these traits don't just happen overnight? They take desire, discipline, and determination. Make a vow to yourself that you will reach out and ask someone to hold you accountable. Choose someone who is honest and will not let you slide. Who is the person you will contact? Will you do it today?

THE JESUS FAST

The accounts of Jesus in the Gospels never fail to inspire and encourage me. The passion and focus He had for His mission is what moves me to want to be like Him. Whether He was in the wilderness praying and fasting or He was standing up to the religious leaders, Jesus was bold.

Fasting is a spiritual act that brings increased willpower and breakthrough. As you fast today, ask God to show you areas in which you need self-control and freedom. Do not be bound to your old thoughts and memory patterns that have held you captive. Be free to be all God created you to be. Your fast is a holy sacrifice unto God, and He sees your heart. Just as Jesus battled the enemy for His victory, you too must battle the evil that tries to tempt you.

Take time right now to just sit and soak in the presence of Holy Spirit. Don't be in a hurry. Just rest. By spending this time with

Him, you truly take control of your will. You must choose to be with Jesus. Just sit in silence. He is here. He is speaking.

DISCUSSION QUESTIONS

- Abigail was a woman who did not wait for everything to work out. She took matters into her own hands and relied upon her God to pave the way. When we seek the hand of God for direction, He truly does lead—but as we know, that takes self-control. Do you seek guidance and direction from God before you make a decision? If not, are you willing to make that change? God sees the beginning from the end. He knows the best route for you to take. Take a moment now and ask yourself why you don't seek God first— maybe pride, or your own ability, or timing (God is too slow)? Take time now and ask God to forgive your impatience or arrogance in not seeking Him. Slow down and talk with God. Where do you need His help in your life right now?

- Nabal was a prideful man who missed out on helping the future king in his time of need. Even though David had taken care of Nabal's men and provided for them, Nabal still resisted the opportunity to care for David and his men. I believe God gives us people and pathways so we can touch the lives of those around us—but if we are too busy with our own agenda, we miss out. When was a time you missed out on helping someone in need? How can you begin to take steps toward opening your eyes to be the hands and feet of Jesus? Write your answer below.

- David exercised self-control by not taking out Nabal's men, and Abigail exercised self-control by thinking clearly and taking action. Think about the ways and times you have demonstrated self-control in your life. What was the outcome? Take a moment and think about where you are exercising self-control right now. Now, write a word of encouragement to yourself. When we affirm ourselves, we are reminded of the power we have to do what is good and what is right. Keep moving forward. Self-control is key to your success.

PRAYER

Dear Lord, today I discovered the power and benefit of self-control. I admit that I don't always seek You first in my projects and decisions. Lord, I ask for Your power to lead and guide me on my life journey. I need discipline and accountability in my life. Help me to control my words and thoughts so I can clearly see Your plan for my life. In Jesus' name, amen.

JOURNAL ENTRY

_____

_____

_____

_____

day
20

FASTING FOR GENEROSITY

THE POOR WIDOW

A lack of generosity refuses to acknowledge that

your assets are not really yours, but God's.

—TIM KELLER

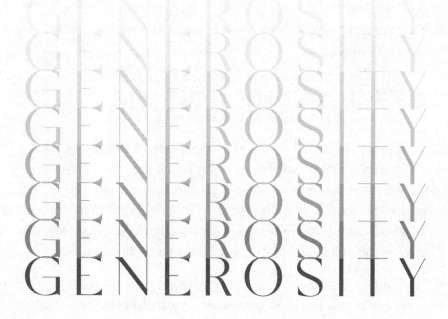

gen·er·os·i·ty | jə-nə-ˈrä-sə-tē |

noun

the quality or fact of being plentiful or large

SIGNS OF LACK OF GENEROSITY

- You're selfish with things that belong to you.
- You have an excess of possessions.
- You think everyone wants something from you.
- You don't look for ways to help others.
- You compare yourself with others' success.

WHEN OTHERS BLESS you with a gift or a much-needed resource, you are moved and grateful. I do believe some people have the spiritual gift of giving, but I also believe it is a behavior we can all aspire to learn and participate in. Scripture is full of stories that illustrate the heart of generosity. Today's focus illuminates how a heart of giving can change both those who are receiving and those who are observing.

SCRIPTURE PASSAGE

Our Scripture passage today is arguably the greatest example of generosity we have, next to Christ's own sacrifice on the cross. As you read it, hear it as a summons to be truly generous. Keep in mind the goal of the fast is to realign your relationship with God precisely so you can ultimately be a blessing for others. This fast may be between you and God, but its implications reach much further.

> He said to them in His teaching, "Beware of the scribes, who love to go about in long robes and love greetings in the

marketplaces, and the prominent seats in the synagogues, and the places of honor at banquets, who devour widows' houses and for a pretense make long prayers. They will receive greater condemnation."

Jesus sat opposite the treasury and saw how the people put money into the treasury. Many who were rich put in much. But a certain poor widow came and put in two mites, which make a farthing. He called His disciples to Him and said to them, "Truly I say to you, this poor widow has put in more than all those who are contributing to the treasury. They all contributed out of their abundance. But she, out of her poverty, put in all that she had, her entire livelihood."

—MARK 12:38–44, MEV

GOING DEEPER

Generosity is a beautiful word to describe the way God loves and provides for His children. It is in our acts of kindness and giving that we are most like Christ, the ultimate Giver. Today's story is both inspiring and challenging because it causes us to dig deep and truly examine the intentions of our hearts. As we read about this widow, we learn several things: she was poor, she was unmarried, she gave all she had, and her life was a testimony to others.

Let's start at the beginning. Jesus was teaching His disciples by warning them to beware the scribes and religious leaders who walked in pride and arrogance, looking for the best seats and high places to be seen by men. He went on to say they take advantage of widows in their homes and offer lofty and pious prayers to intimidate people.

As the disciples sat holding on to every word He spoke, Jesus took the opportunity to teach them a lesson. The treasury was the place where Jews would donate and contribute to the aid of temple ministry and upkeep. As Jesus and His disciples sat gazing at the treasury, they saw people stopping to make donations.

"Look," Jesus said. "Do you see everyone stopping to place their offerings into the treasury?"

They answered, "Yes, of course, Jesus. That is what we are commanded to do: help those in need."

"Yes," Jesus replied, "but did you see the widow who followed behind? She put in two mites. Who do you think gave more?" Simple math would say those who put in large amounts put in the greater gift. But no, Jesus said—for those who are rich give out of their excess, but the widow gives out of her poverty. She indeed gave the greater gift.

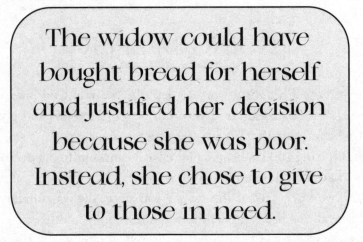

> The widow could have bought bread for herself and justified her decision because she was poor. Instead, she chose to give to those in need.

The interesting thing about the widow is that she could have walked down a different road. She could have bought bread for herself and justified her decision because she was poor. Instead, this widow went on purpose with kindness in her heart to give to those in need.

We can all think of times when others were generous, gracious, and kind toward us. I will never forget one such memory.

My husband and I were young and still in seminary when we had our two boys. Now, it goes without saying that we did not have much revenue coming in. We went to school Tuesday through Friday and then made our way to our church on the weekend. At the time, we had two young boys in diapers. Name-brand diapers were definitely a luxury, but one we tried to budget for. As we drove off the seminary campus, I mentioned to my husband that we would need to stop and pick up diapers for the boys. He replied that funds were tight and we would have to wait until we got to our destination, where we could buy the diapers on our tab at the local general store. I distinctly remember him saying, "You'd better just pray the boys don't have an accident on the way there." I did not laugh—but I did pray.

I remember praying something like, "God, we are in Your service. We are pastors with two small children. We have a need, and You can supply it." To be honest, I was not sure that I'd prayed sincerely, and I was not sure if He even heard me.

As we pulled into the driveway of our small church home, we noticed a large box on the porch. I assumed the youth of our church were playing another trick on us. (We were not much older than our youth group. They thought we were cool and fun, and they loved to play pranks on us.)

After getting the boys situated in the house, my husband opened the front door to check out the large container. To our surprise, it was a case of diapers—not a box, a case. *Thirty-two boxes.* It seems the owner of the local general store had taken a liking to my husband and said he was the only preacher up there at that church that was honest. He did not attend a church, but his wife did. When he asked her what he could do for the young preacher and his wife, she said, "Well, they have two babies; what do you think?" He decided to order us a case of diapers. And as you can see, we are still telling the story of this man's generosity today. He saw a need and he met it.

The beautiful thing about generosity is its reciprocal nature—sometimes we receive it and sometimes we give it, but most times we get to bear witness. The widow's mite lives on today as a story about generosity and giving from a pure heart. Is your story of doing good being told by someone today? We learn from today's story that God sees our heart and our motive. It is only in sacrificial giving that we are most like Jesus. Giving to others, nonprofits, or even your local church is a good thing—and the Word of God instructs us to do so—but it is those who give out of their poverty and sacrifice who are remembered.

FOR FURTHER STUDY

Your fast is a time to cultivate generosity. The following verses are an invitation to a generous life. Read them prayerfully and be open to whatever action the Holy Spirit is calling you to take in light of them.

- 1 John 3:17
- Hebrews 13:16
- Luke 6:38
- Luke 12:32
- Proverbs 19:17
- Proverbs 28:27
- Psalm 112:9

COACHING STEPS

1. You know whether you are generous or not. The question is, do you want to be? Generosity starts with wanting to bless others. It is also contagious. Start each

day by committing to do something for someone else. Buy someone's coffee or lunch. Surprise someone with flowers or an act of service. Take in your neighbor's trash cans. It does not have to cost you money, but it does require your time and your attention. Becoming generous will change your attitude as well as the attitudes of those whom you bless.

2. The act of generosity can cause you to become prideful. You must examine your heart and ask yourself why you are doing what you are doing. Consider our scripture today—the religious leaders performed acts of kindness only to be seen by others. Their hearts were full of false piety and arrogance. True kindness will flow from a pure heart. The goal of this lesson is for you to become more like Christ and see the needs of others with a heart of compassion. Once you begin to give unto others, you will love how it makes you feel—grateful for all you have. An easy way to train yourself in generosity is to put acts of kindness on your daily calendar. This will train you to develop a lifestyle of generosity.

3. Jesus used the act of the widow as a teaching lesson for His disciples. I fear we have become so self-absorbed today that we don't even see the needs of those around us. Homelessness, brokenness, and emptiness are all around us. If you were to actually stop and count the number of people you come across each day who need your help, I suspect you would be surprised. The truth is that many of us have become immune to those in need. Take some time today and look for ways to be kind, generous, and giving. Jesus just might use you as a teaching lesson today.

THE JESUS FAST

How are you doing on your fast? We are almost finished with our twenty-one days together, and I would like to ask you a question: Have you drawn closer to God over these last three weeks? Jesus taught us the spiritual discipline of fasting so we could open doors for breakthrough and grow in our intimacy with Him.

On your fast today, take time to reevaluate the topics we have examined together. Have you asked God to help you become more like Him? Have you made personal changes in your life to develop healthy habits and Christlike behavior?

Today we have considered generosity. As we have seen from our Jesus fast, there is no one more generous than our Lord Jesus. He gave all to those who had nothing. To whom can you be like Christ today? Whom can you help, assist, or minister to today? Be generous with your time and your resources, and people will be blessed by your actions.

DISCUSSION QUESTIONS

- What are you feeling after today's teaching? Do you feel guilty, excited, or convicted? Both in Jesus' day and our own, people have needs and want help. What are some ways you can assist the people around you today? Make a commitment to do something intentionally. In the space below, write down the acts of kindness and generosity you feel God prompting you to carry out.

- In our coaching tips for today I mentioned that one way to train yourself to be generous is to place ideas on your calendar. Take some time right now and list a few things you can do this week such as running an errand for someone, buying a coffee for a colleague, taking in your neighbor's trash can, or sending a greeting card to a friend. These are just a few ideas, but once you start the generosity train in your life, you will not want to stop.

• We have been fasting for several weeks now. One of the blessings of fasting is taking the time to examine our hearts and focus more of our attention on the things of God. How has this fast caused you to see things differently? What are you asking God to do in your life today? Being aware of the world around you will open your eyes to see the heart of God in a much deeper dimension.

PRAYER

Dear Lord, today I learned about the power of generosity—not only for my benefit but also for those who are observing my actions. Lord, I desire to be more Christlike. Teach me to see the needs of others and to do my part in helping humanity. I commit to making the effort to do acts of kindness and be more generous with my life. In Jesus' name, amen.

JOURNAL ENTRY

_____

_____

_____

_____

_____

_____

_____

_____

_____

_____

_____

_____

_____

_____

_____

_____

day
21

FASTING FOR
HUMILITY

JESUS

Humility is not a character trait to develop; it's the natural by-product of being with Jesus.

—LOUIE GIGLIO

Humility and patience are the surest proofs of the increase of love.

—JOHN WESLEY

hu·mil·i·ty | hyü-ˈmi-lə-tē |

noun

a modest or low view of one's own importance; humbleness

SIGNS OF LACK OF HUMILITY

- You talk too much about yourself.
- You are consumed with your schedule.
- You are not willing to admit when you are wrong.
- You use humor at others' expense.
- You walk with arrogance and pride.

WHAT IS HUMILITY? I think this quote from the late John R. W. Stott—who was said to have had the greatest impact for Christ of anyone in the twentieth century—pretty much sums it up: "Pride is your greatest enemy, humility is your greatest friend."[1]

On our last day together, we are going to look at the greatest act of humility known to man: the divine sacrifice of Jesus dying on a rugged and brutal cross for the sin of humanity.

SCRIPTURE PASSAGES

Pilate said to them, "Then what shall I do with Jesus who is called Christ?"

They all said to him, "Let Him be crucified!"

The governor said, "Why, what evil has He done?"

But they cried out all the more, "Let Him be crucified!"

When Pilate saw that he could not prevail, but rather that unrest was beginning, he took water and washed his hands before the crowd, saying, "I am innocent of the blood of this righteous Man. See to it yourselves."

Then all the people answered, "His blood be on us and on our children!"...

Then the soldiers of the governor took Jesus into the Praetorium, and gathered the whole detachment of soldiers before Him. They stripped Him and put a scarlet robe on Him, and when they wove a crown of thorns, they put it on His head and put a staff in His right hand. They knelt before Him and mocked Him, saying, "Hail, King of the Jews!" They spit on Him, and took the staff and hit Him on the head. After they had mocked Him, they took the robe off Him, put His own garments on Him, and led Him away to crucify Him....

Those who passed by insulted Him, wagging their heads, saying, "You who would destroy the temple and build it in three days, save Yourself! If You are the Son of God, come down from the cross." Likewise the chief priests, with the scribes and elders, mocked Him, saying, "He saved others. He cannot save Himself. If He is the King of Israel, let Him now come down from the cross, and we will believe Him. He trusted in God. Let Him deliver Him now, if He will have Him. For He said, 'I am the Son of God.'"

—MATTHEW 27:22–25, 27–31, 39–43, MEV

Let this mind be in you which was also in Christ Jesus, who, being in the form of God, did not consider it robbery to be equal with God, but made Himself of no reputation, taking the form of a bondservant, and coming in the likeness of men. And being found in appearance as a man, He humbled Himself and became obedient to the point of death, even the death of the cross. Therefore God also has highly exalted Him and given Him the name which is above every name, that at the name of Jesus every knee should bow, of those in heaven, and of those on earth, and of those under the earth, and that every tongue should confess that Jesus Christ is Lord, to the glory of God the Father.

—PHILIPPIANS 2:5–11

GOING DEEPER

Over our past several days together we have looked at various characteristics and behavior traits we all aspire to possess, and I believe today's topic is paramount to them all because it stems from a heart of love. Jesus was bold and brilliant, yet He was surely the greatest example of humility ever known. He did not act with pride or arrogance at any point in His ministry. That is why so many people followed Him—they were attracted to His humility.

Given the humility we see on display in the life and ministry of Jesus, it is hard, then, to read these passages and not become angry at the people's injustice. Yet we see all the ways the humility of God was embodied in Jesus precisely through the way He responded to all of this injustice. There is no explanation for why Jesus would have endured the ridicule and pain of Calvary other than from a heart of humility and love. This is not something we can work up or develop; rather, it is something only God can give us. It is only in the light of the love of Jesus that we can truly live humble lives.

Consider all the ways that Jesus demonstrated His radical humility, even when it led to His death. First, Jesus was stripped and mocked as the crowd placed a scarlet robe around Him. Next, the people placed a crown of thorns on His head and a reed in His hand while laughing and taunting Him with shouts of His royal position, yet Jesus did not say a word. Then the crowd led Jesus away to be crucified in shame and belittlement, all the while spitting on Him and chanting, "If You are the King of the Jews, save Yourself now. What's wrong, Jesus? You can save the world, but You cannot save Yourself?"

In a matter of moments we see condemnation, ridicule, hatred, betrayal, pain, and punishment—all the while, Jesus never opened His mouth. He could have called heaven down to rebuke them, or stopped them with the power of His word, or even called on

His Father to destroy them all—but no, not a word. Such was His humility for the greater cause. Such was the depth of His love for humanity.

We are living in a time of self-indulgence, entitlement, pride, and prosperity. Humility is the furthest thing from our minds. Are we really any different from our first-century family? The heart of humanity will always seek out our own agenda, looking to comfort our souls with thoughts of justification. The people in Jesus' day convinced themselves they were doing the right thing by accusing and scapegoating another as we also convince ourselves we are doing the right thing today. Yet Jesus was undeterred—He still purposely walked the road of humility as an act of love and devotion for His children.

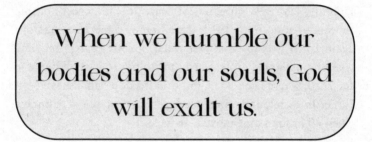

When we humble our bodies and our souls, God will exalt us.

Humility looks like weakness to some people because it does not seek its own agenda. Humility is gentle and kind, compassionate and long-suffering. Yet as we see in the life of Jesus, humility is also attractive and appealing. The very crowds that crucified Him were the same people who sought out His teaching after He was resurrected. The self-sacrificial humility Jesus displayed on the cross looked like defeat at the time, but it was actually the very power that overcame the forces of sin and death. Walking in humility means playing the long game now as it did then.

Humility is grounded in the nature of God. It is who He is. In the words of Psalm 25:9, "He leads the humble in what is right, and teaches the humble his way" (ESV).

For all the ways that fasting is beneficial, none is as significant as this: fasting helps usher us into the kind of Christlike humility that allows us to experience the full victory of God. When we humble our bodies and our souls, God will exalt us.

In the same way that walking the path of humility was crucial to Jesus' defeating Satan and his forces, it is crucial for us now. The One who carried the cross for us in humility calls us to take up our own cross and follow Him. Fasting helps us enter into the cross-shaped humility through which we find the power to overcome. With this in view, as we conclude our twenty-one days together, may this reflection by Andrew Murray be the aim of your life:

> Humility is perfect quietness of heart. It is to expect nothing, to wonder at nothing that is done to me, to feel nothing done against me. It is to be at rest when nobody praises me, and when I am blamed or despised. It is to have a blessed home in the Lord, where I can go in and shut the door, and kneel to my Father in secret, and am at peace as in a deep sea of calmness, when all around and above is trouble.[2]

FOR FURTHER STUDY

As we conclude our fast, the Spirit invites us to embrace this most quintessentially Christlike trait, the thing that defined Him most to the people around Him: His humility. The greatest gift of fasting is that it humbles us, putting us back in touch with our humanity, frailty, vulnerability, and dependence so that we are once again open to the surprise of God. As you read the following passages, ask God to embed in you the deep humility of Christ Himself.

- James 4:10

- Ephesians 4:2

- Micah 6:8

- 1 Peter 3:8

- Exodus 10:3

- Proverbs 16:19

- Luke 1:52

- 2 Chronicles 7:14

COACHING STEPS

1. As we mentioned, humility is not something we can acquire but something we choose. Only through the love and grace of God can we ever possess the attribute of humility. You must begin by recognizing your own shortcomings and limitations. Allow the Holy Spirit of God to fill you with His love for others. We must see humanity through the eyes of God.

2. It is important that we value others and recognize their strengths and abilities. Humility looks out for the well-being of others. It lays the foundation for others to travel on. One of the greatest blessings of wisdom and maturity is discipling those who will follow. It is not haughty or puffed up, but humble and kind.

3. Another dimension of humility is that a humble person is open to learning from others. Always have a teachable spirit. Proverbs 9:9 tells us, "Give instruction to a wise man, and he will be still wiser; teach

a righteous man, and he will increase in learning" (esv). You will never stop learning or growing in the knowledge of God. Be receptive to the teaching of others.

THE JESUS FAST

I chose this topic for the Jesus fast, for there is none more humble than our Lord and Savior, Jesus Christ. We see the evidence of His humility from His temptation in the wilderness to the curse of the crucifixion and in everything in between. As we end our fast together today, it is my prayer that you have pressed into the depths of God on our journey and into the humility of Christ. I hope you have been encouraged to seek the attributes and qualities that will make you the person God created you to be.

As you fast today, recommit yourself to this humble King. Decide that you will be wholly devoted to the Lord and His plans for your life. Make your fast a sacrifice unto Him alone. Keep your eyes and your heart fixed upon His Word and allow Him to lead you all the days of your life—one day at a time.

DISCUSSION QUESTIONS

- Have you ever asked yourself, "If I were living in Jesus' day, would I have been for Him or against Him"? It's a good question, and not one to rush past. Would you have sat at His teachings or looked for a way to find fault in Him? It is easy to think we would have been followers of Christ, but are we actually following Jesus' teaching now?

- This story reminds us of the great love the Father has for us. He sent His Son to redeem humanity, even at the cost of crucifixion. Take a moment now and thank Jesus for His great love for you. Sit for a moment and just let it sink in. You are loved and redeemed.

- We learned that humility is not something we can earn or possess on our own—we receive it from Christ. How would you assess your level of humility based on our teaching today? What are some ways you can incorporate the lifestyle of Jesus to walk the road of humility? What step will you take today?

- We have fasted for twenty-one days together. As we have learned from our teaching videos, fasting is an act of our will and a sacrifice unto the Lord. It is more than abstaining from food; it is holy unto the Lord. What breakthroughs or blessings have you seen because of your fast? Is fasting something you will commit to doing on a regular basis? Share your thoughts below.

PRAYER

Dear Lord, my journey with You over the last twenty-one days has been enlightening and revealing. It is my prayer that I will pursue the qualities and attributes that You have created in me. I know that I am made in the image of God and that I have the power to walk in the fullness of Your Spirit. Teach me to be an example of Your humility and kindness to the world. Help me to hear Your voice and obey Your ways. In Jesus' name, amen.

JOURNAL ENTRY

DAY 02

1. Marcel Schwantes, "Science says only 8 percent of people actually achieve their goals. Here are 7 things they do differently," Inc.com, June 13, 2018, https://www.inc.com/marcel-schwantes/science-says-only-8-percent-of-people-actually-achieve-their-goals-here-are-7-things-they-do-differently.html.

DAY 04

1. *Merriam-Webster*, s.v. "faith," accessed August 11, 2023, https://www.merriam-webster.com/dictionary/faith.

DAY 07

1. Kay Picolet, "Loyalty—'A Strong Feeling of Support or Allegiance,'" JP Gasway, January 22, 2019, http://www.jpgasway.com/blog/2019/1/22/loyalty-a-strong-feeling-of-support-or-allegiance.

DAY 09

1. "Aristotle Quotes," Goodreads.com, accessed August 11, 2023, https://www.goodreads.com/quotes/752499-there-is-a-foolish-corner-in-the-brain-of-the.

DAY 11

1. "Helen Keller Quotes," BrainyQuote.com, accessed August 11, 2023, https://www.brainyquote.com/quotes/helen_keller_383771.

DAY 12

1. Sarah A. Schnitker and Robert A. Emmons, "Patience as a virtue: Religious and psychological perspectives," *Research in the Social Scientific Study of Religion* vol. 18: 177–207, https://brill.com/display/book/edcoll/9789047419648/Bej.9789004158511.i-301_012.xml.

NOTES

DAY 14

1. Victor Lipman, "Surprising, Disturbing Facts From the Mother of All Employee Engagement Surveys," Forbes, September 23, 2013, https://www.forbes.com/sites/victorlipman/2013/09/23/surprising-disturbing-facts-from-the-mother-of-all-employee-engagement-surveys/?sh=4f66b5db3120.

DAY 15

1. C. S. Lewis, *Mere Christianity* (Grand Rapids, MI: HarperCollins, 2009), 50.

DAY 16

1. *Merriam-Webster*, s.v. "discipline," accessed August 11, 2023, https://www.merriam-webster.com/dictionary/discipline.

DAY 21

1. Thomas A. Tarrants, "Pride and Humility," C. S. Lewis Institute, December 4, 2011, https://www.cslewisinstitute.org/resources/pride-and-humility/.
2. Andrew Murray quoted in John M. Perkins, *He Calls Me Friend: The Healing Power of Friendship in a Lonely World* (Chicago: Moody Publishers, 2019), 47.

TAMMY HOTSENPILLER IS an eleven-time author, a speaker, a life coach, and the leader of a national women's movement. She has a passion for equipping people to embrace their natural abilities, personal passions, and spiritual gifts. She is the president of Total Life Coach and the founder of Women of Influence (woi.today). Hotsenpiller is a much-sought-after speaker, social media influencer, and podcast host.

She and her husband, Phil, are the cofounders of Influence Church in Anaheim Hills, California. They live in Orange County, California, and are blessed with three amazing children, their equally incredible spouses, and eight grandchildren.

TAMMYHOTSENPILLER.COM

ABOUT the AUTHOR